Y0-DKP-719

The Complete Book
of Baseball Drills

The Complete Book
of Baseball Drills

Robert G. Hoehn

Parker Publishing Company, Inc.
West Nyack, New York

© 1977 by

PARKER PUBLISHING COMPANY, INC.
West Nyack, New York

Library of Congress Cataloging in Publication Data

Hoehn, Robert G
   The complete book of baseball drills.

   Includes index.
   1. Baseball. I. Title.
GV867.3.H63   796.357'2   76-56255
ISBN 0-13-155978-8

Printed in the United States of America

To Peggy, Valerie, Susan, and James

ACKNOWLEDGEMENTS

I wish to thank Robert Vlasak for his fine illustrations that appear throughout the book.

A special thanks to Clyde Bearden for his time and interest in preparing the excellent photographs.

I express my appreciation to Bill Peterson and Mike Manfredi, the outstanding athletes appearing in the photographs.

HOW THIS BOOK CAN HELP YOU

Two problems that face most of us as baseball coaches are:
(1) What activities to include in practice; (2) How to keep every
player busy during practice. THE COMPLETE BOOK OF BASE-
BALL DRILLS gives you exercises, drills, and games for each athlete that stress the skills necessary for successful team play. Each
drill includes objective, procedure, time, notes and comments (when
applicable). This practical guide works hand in hand with you, the
coach, by:

- Providing over 175 activities that help players improve
  throughout the season.
- Arousing player interest and motivation through competitive
  games. Game-like activities appear throughout the book.
  For example, Chapter 7: *Keeping Players Sharp with Competitive Team Games,* presents 10 drills that give each
  athlete a chance to polish his hitting, bunting, fielding,
  throwing, and base running techniques.
- Permitting athletes to work in small groups. Chapter 3:
  Employing Fast-Moving Drills for Small Groups, offers 6
  drills for 3 players; 5 drills for 4 players; 4 drills for 5 players;
  and 4 drills for 6 players.
- Presenting a unit (Chapter 9) on how to organize indoor
  drills and games during inclement weather.
- Giving several examples on how to set up daily practice
  schedules using the drills, exercises, and games described in
  this book (Chapter 12).
- Describing aggressive sliding drills and games for every
  player (Chapter 8).
- Describing game-winning team offensive and defensive
  strategy (Chapter 11).

- Offering early season exercises and drills for pitchers. Chapter 1 presents 24 drills, plus sections on stretching exercises, running, muscle strengthening exercises, and workout schedules for the first 3 weeks of practice. Chapter 2: *Utilizing Early Season Exercises and Drills for All Players,* gives 15 excellent conditioning activities.
- Including chapters on how athletes can improve their fielding, throwing, and hitting.

The book closes with a chapter on games every player will enjoy. Photographs, charts, and illustrations have been carefully selected to help you prepare your daily practice schedule.

Robert G. Hoehn

TABLE OF CONTENTS

Chapter 7: Keeping Players Sharp with Competitive Team Games
(cont.)

Chapter 8: Aggressive Sliding Drills and Games for Every Player — 171

Chapter 9: Employing Indoor Drills and Games During Inclement Weather — 187

Chapter 10: Drills for Players with Fielding, Throwing, and Hitting Problems — 205

Chapter 11: Game-Winning Offensive and Defensive Drills — 217

Chapter 12: Setting Up the Practice Session — 229

Chapter 13: Games Your Players Will Enjoy — 233

Index — 249

1

Developing Pitchers with Early Season Exercises and Drills

There are several factors that determine how successful a pitcher will be. These include mental attitude, physical condition, alertness, quickness, and the ability to execute fundamentals. A pitcher, to be effective, must do many stretching, strengthening, and running exercises throughout the season.

Many pitchers look good at the start of the season, then for some mysterious reason, gradually or suddenly, they lose their stuff. They begin to worry about the fast ball "everybody" hits or the hanging curve ball that sailed high over the scoreboard. Why the turnabout? Pitchers, like batters, suffer from periodic slumps. These often happen to the hurler who believes a conditioning program is no longer needed after the first three weeks of practice.

The exercises and drills described in this chapter will help you to plan an early season program for your pitchers. These activities can be repeated throughout the season.

Let's begin with six stretching exercises.

Stretching Exercises

1. Full Extension

Objective — To stretch the arm, leg, and stomach muscles.

Procedure — Lie flat on back. (Figure 1A.) Fully extend arms and legs. (Figure 1B.) Reach out as far as possible. Hold position for 5 seconds. Return to resting position. Repeat 10 times. Add 2 repetitions every 3 days.

Comment — The type of exercises and number of repetitions vary with coaching philosophy.

(FIGURE 1 A.)

(FIGURE 1 B.)

2. Back Stretch

Objective — To stretch the arm, leg, and back muscles.

Procedure — Stand straight with feet spread apart shoulder-width. (Figure 2A.) Hold arms straight and close to the body.

Bend at the waist. Reach toward the heels with both arms. (Figure 2B.) Keep legs straight while reaching back. Hold position for 5 seconds. Return to standing position. Repeat 5 or 6 times, stretching a little farther each time. Add 2 repetitions every 3 days.

(FIGURE 2A.)

(FIGURE 2B.)

3. Sitting Position

Objective — To stretch the thigh and leg muscles.

Procedure — Stand with back flat against a solid structure, e.g., wall, door, fence or tree. Hold back firmly against structure and slowly lower body to a sit-down position. Let arms hang alongside of the body. (Figure 3.) Hold position for approximately 10 seconds. Return to standing position. Repeat several times.

(FIGURE 3)

4. Lean Back

Objective — To stretch the thigh, back, and buttocks muscles.
Procedure — Stand erect. Spread legs apart shoulder-width. Point toes toward each other. Place hands on hips. Bend knees, lean back, and keep body weight on inside of feet. (Figures 4A and 4B.) Use the thigh and buttocks muscles to move body up and down. Repeat 10 times. Add 2 repetitions every 3 days.

5. Pull In

Objective — To stretch inside thigh muscles.
Procedure — Stand erect. Spread legs apart shoulder-width. Point toes toward each other. Place hands on hips. Lower body by using thigh muscles. (Figure 5.) Return to standing position. Repeat 10 times. Add 2 repetitions every 3 days.

(FIGURE 4A.)   (FIGURE 4B.)

(FIGURE 5)

6. Bar Hang

Objective — To stretch the arm muscles.

Procedure — Hang from an overhead bar with both hands. Keep both feet off the ground. Let arms support body weight. (Figure 6A.) Release the non-pitching hand from the bar. (Figure 6B.) Hold body weight for about 10 seconds. Repeat 2 or 3 times daily.

(FIGURE 6A.)   (FIGURE 6B.)

Many coaches make stretching exercises a daily part of their programs. They know the importance of preparing back, arm, tricep, hamstring, quadricep and groin muscles for competition. Here is a partial list of additional stretching exercises:

Knees Over — Lie back against floor. Grab hips with both hands. Gradually bring knees over head. Touch shoulders with knees. Hold for 5 seconds. Return to resting position. Repeat several times.

Knee Spread — Lie back against floor. Hold legs and feet together. Keep hands alongside body. Draw knees toward chest. Spread knees far apart. Hold for 5 seconds. Return to resting position. Repeat several times.

Shift Back — Assume push-up position. Shift weight to toes by pushing body toward feet. Hold for 5 seconds. Return to resting position. Repeat several times.

Reach — Assume sit-down position. Hold legs and feet together. Extend both arms and reach for toes. Stretch as far as possible. Hold for 5 seconds. Return to resting position. Repeat several times.

You cannot assume that your pitchers do their loosening exercises faithfully before practice. One way to stress proper conditioning is to hold a pre-season meeting. At this meeting each player should receive a training handbook listing those exercises and drills that you feel are important. You can explain these activities to the new players while returning players demonstrate their proper execution.

Running

Running is a vital part of any athletic program and a pitcher must do plenty of running to get his legs into shape. Running, together with stretching and bending exercises, helps build endurance and develop speed.

Many coaches prefer to have their pitchers run wind sprints at the end of practice. These are some of the methods that can be used:

- Run ten 30-yard sprints. Use run-walk, run-walk sequence. Distance is increased and more sprints added as pitchers get into shape.
- Run ten 50-yard sprints. Players start from a standing or sprinter's position. Use run-walk, run-walk sequence. Distance is increased and more sprints added as pitchers get into shape.
- Sprint 100 yards at one-half speed. Use walk or jog return. Gradually increase pace to three quarters and full speed. The number of repetitions is optional.

- Fifteen minute sprint. Pitchers run at three-quarters speed for 15 minutes in this manner: run 6 minutes, walk 3 minutes, and run the remaining 6 minutes. As pitchers get into shape, they run 12 minutes and rest 3 minutes.
- Run up the bleachers or stands at close to full speed. The number of repetitions is optional (usually from 20 to 35).
- Run from one to three miles around the track. Sprint the straight a way and walk or jog the turns.

A wise coach will combine fielding drills with running activities. He knows that his players need variety to sustain interest. Here are four leg strengthening drills that fit well into the program.

7. Leg and Peg

Objective — To practice running and fielding.
Procedure — Pitchers pair off. They stand about 40 yards apart and face each other. Pitcher A brings a ball, bat, and glove to Station 1. When he hollers "Go," Pitcher B runs at full speed toward him. Pitcher B stops at Station 1, picks up the glove, and runs at half-speed toward Station 2. Pitcher A tosses a fly ball or hits a grounder to the right or to the left of Player B. Player B fields the ball. (Figure 7.) He returns the ball and glove to Station 2. Player A then becomes the runner and fielder. Each athlete receives 10 to 15 chances to run and field.
Comment — Turn *Leg and Peg* into a game. A player earns one point each time he makes a clean play. He receives no points if he misses or bobbles the ball. The athlete collecting the most points wins.
Time — 15 to 20 minutes.

8. Bat and Sprint

Objective — To practice running and fielding.
Procedure — This drill follows the same procedure as *Leg and Peg* with one exception: Pitchers A and B bring a bat, ball, and glove to their stations. Instead of tossing a ball, each player takes turns hitting the ball to the other.

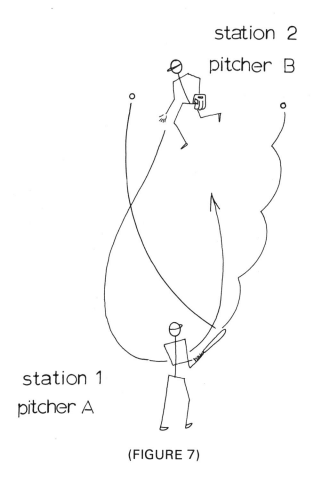

station 2

pitcher B

station 1

pitcher A

(FIGURE 7)

For example, Pitcher B (wearing a glove) runs to Station 1, rounds it, and heads back toward Station 2. Pitcher A fungos* a ball to Player B. Action continues with each athlete fielding 10 to 15 balls. Keep game points the same as in *Leg and Peg.*

Time — 15 to 20 minutes.

The popular pick-up drill requires a pitcher to keep his body low and field baseballs tossed to his left and to his right. He fields between 25 to 50 balls before switching with his partner. *Shadow* and *Zig-Zag* are variations of pick-up.

---

*Hoehn, Robert G. "Fungolf for Baseball Relaxation," *The Coaching Clinic,* Vol. 10, No. 2, February, 1972, pp. 2-4.

9. Shadow

Objective — To strengthen the legs.

Procedure — Three pitchers form a group. They position them-selves according to Figure 8. Player 1 places himself about 25 to 30 feet in front of Player 2. Player 3 stays approximately 6 to 8 feet directly behind Player 2.

Action begins when Player 1, feeder, tosses a ball to one side of Player 2. Player 2 fields and makes an underhand return to Player 1. Player 3, shadow, stays behind Player 2 and simulates fielding the ball. Play continues as Player 2, running from side to side, fields 25 to 50 balls. Player 2 then becomes Player 3, Player 3 becomes Player 1, and Player 1 becomes Player 2.

Comment — Urge athletes to make an all-out effort. Tell players to use both hands when fielding the ball. Suggestion: Have pitchers do 25 pick-ups during the first few days of practice. Gradually increase number to 50 and 75.

Time — 15 to 20 minutes.

10. Zig-Zag

Objective — To strengthen the legs.

Procedure — A pitcher brings a glove and ball onto the field. He starts play by tossing the ball 15 to 20 feet to one side. After the ball comes to rest, he sprints over and picks it up with both hands. He continues action by tossing the ball to his opposite side. The pitcher repeats throw-ing the ball from side to side 25 to 50 times.

Time — 10 to 15 minutes.

Muscle Strengthening Exercises

Pitchers, as well as other team members, need to build muscle tone. A carefully planned weight and exercise training program prior to regular season will help athletes develop strength and power. Starting weight exercises may include wrist curls, bench presses, half squats or leg presses, and sit-ups. The player gradually adds more weight as he gains strength.

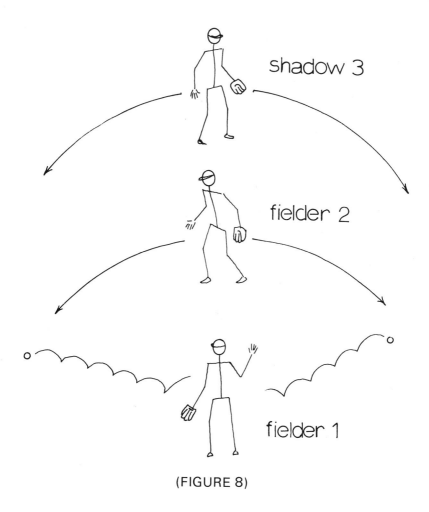

(FIGURE 8)

Following is a simple program for a healthy, reasonably strong player who has never done any previous weight training*.

Exercises	Suggested Starting Weight
Clean and press	One-third of body weight plus 10 pounds
Sit-ups	Light weights (10-20 lbs.)
Bench press	One-half of body weight

---

*Rowen, Tom. "Let the Experts Speak," *Baseball Conditioning*. Dorrance and Company, Philadelphia, PA., 1973, pp. 30-31.

Half squat or
  leg press   One-half of body weight plus 10 pounds
  Curls   One-third of body weight plus 10 pounds

A three set program of ten, eight, and six repetitions for each exercise is best for the beginner. A player learns to lift weight properly while his muscles become accustomed to strenuous exercise. When soreness leaves and when ten repetitions can be performed with the third set, all three sets are increased by ten pounds. For example, suppose the player is on a ten, eight, six program of 40, 50, and 60 pounds. When he becomes able to lift 60 pounds ten times, he is allowed to change his weights to 50, 60, and 70 pounds. When the 70 pounds can be lifted ten times on the third set, his weights will be changed to 60, 70, and 80 pounds.

Alternate day programs when players do not lift should fit the individual needs of each player. During poor weather, players can work indoors. Pitchers can practice throwing and hitters should swing the lead bat at least 100 times a day. Basketball and badminton are excellent off-day games.

A pitcher can strengthen his wrists, hands, and fingers with chin-ups, rope climbing, lifting or rolling a weight on a handle, finger-tip push-ups, and squeezing a rubber ball.

Exercise	Number	Comments
Push-ups	20	Add 2 every 3 practices
Fingertip push-ups	15	Add 2 every 3 practices
Pull-ups or chin-ups	8	Add 2 every 3 practices
Sit-ups	20	Add 2 every 3 practices
Squat thrusts	15	Add 2 every 3 practices
Rope climb	10	Add 2 every 3 practices

The type of alternate-day exercises and the number of repetitions depend on facilities, time, and coaching discretion. Suggestions: Alternate push-ups with pull-ups. These are excellent shoulder joint strengtheners. If possible, include rope climbing. Alternate chin-ups, dips on parallel bars, and push-ups. These exercises strengthen the elbow muscles.

Encourage athletes to work hard, but never ask a player to go beyond his physical capacity. An athlete may not be able to exceed

14 push-ups or 6 pull-ups. Let the athlete set limits for himself. Be ready to offer assistance.

Throwing

An early season program should include easy throwing while the pitcher is getting his legs into shape. The following activities will help a pitcher ready his arm for competition.

11. Easy Toss

Objective — To gradually warm-up the pitching arm.
Procedure — Pitchers pair off and stand about 60 feet apart. They take turns pitching and catching balls thrown at half speed. The receiving player gives the hurler a target by holding his glove still. The hurler concentrates on hitting the glove.
Comment — Pitchers gradually add speed to each pitch until they are throwing at three-quarter speed. After a few days, have pitchers pair off with catchers and continue working on control. Suggestion: Caution pitchers to throw only straight balls at first. Throwing too many curve balls early in the season places heavy strain on arm muscles. A hurler should increase the number of pitches as his arm becomes stronger. For example, if he throws 30 pitches at first, he should increase the number of pitches to 50, then 75, upward to 100.
Time — 20 to 25 minutes.

Figure 9 shows the pitcher holding the ball with a cross-seam grip. Notice how the ball rests between the index finger, middle finger and thumb. The two fingers, slightly spread, give the pitcher a comfortable grip which many pitchers prefer.

Figure 10 shows the ball held with the middle finger pressed along the seam. This grip often causes the ball to slide or slice as it approaches the plate. Some experienced players learn to control a moving pitch, but younger athletes might have trouble throwing strikes. Suggestion: Let the pitcher decide which grip works best for him. (He's going to use it anyway.)

(FIGURE 9)

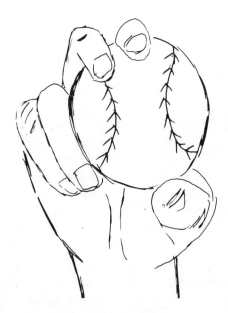

(FIGURE 10)

12. Grip Toss

Objective — To practice using the cross-seam grip.
Procedure — Two pitchers (or pitcher and catcher) pair off and stand approximately 60 feet apart. Each pitcher throws one-half to three-quarter speed using the cross-seam grip. As the hurler's arm loosens up, he mixes throwing fast balls, curve balls and change-ups.

The receiver has an important job. He must carefully watch the pitcher wind up and release the ball. He looks for two things: the pitcher changing grips or the pitcher showing too much baseball. Changing grips for different pitches may affect control; exposing the baseball tips off a smart hitter as to what pitch is coming next.

Here is a simple drill variation that pitchers can use at home: Gather 6 or 7 baseballs. Set a pillow, hanging tire, folded blanket, or baseball glove against a solid support in front of a wall or screen. Practice throwing the ball at the target. Keep eyes fixed on the target. Concentrate on using the same grip with each pitch.
Time — 15 to 25 minutes.

Pitchers use different styles of delivery. These include the overhand, three-quarters, side-arm, and underarm. Many hurlers favor the three-quarters delivery because the arm and body are in excellent position to whip the ball forward. (Figure 11A.)

As the pitcher winds up, he lifts and moves his front foot toward home plate. His body and shoulders work together to carry his arm through an approximate 45° angle. Both feet land facing the batter. Body weight distribution remains under control and the pitcher is ready to field any ball hit his way. (Figure 11B.) The next two drills will help a pitcher develop smooth body motion.

13. Wall Rebound

Objective — To practice the pitching motion.
Procedure — Use tape or string to make a strike zone against a wall or garage door. Stand about 60 feet away. Practice

(FIGURE 11A)   (FIGURE 11B)

throwing a soft rubber ball into the strike zone. Make sure body weight is well under control. Catch returning balls in a low fielding position. Note: Throw at one-half speed. Concentrate on fielding balls out in front of the body.

Comment — This is a good pre-season activity that players can do at home. Caution pitchers to throw easy and follow-through completely with each delivery.

Time — 15 minutes.

14. Catcher Flip

Objective — To practice the pitching motion.

Procedure — Pitchers and catchers pair off and stand about 60 feet away from each other. The pitcher concentrates on throwing strikes to the catcher. After each delivery, the catcher flips the ball to the right, to the left, or

directly in front of the pitcher. The pitcher fields and
again throws the ball to the catcher. The catcher
watches the pitcher carefully. He makes pitching corrections as needed.

Time — 15 to 20 minutes.

Before a pitcher releases the ball, he snaps his wrist. His hand
and fingers combine with the snap to whip the ball forward. The
snap release, with forward body motion, adds power to the pitch.
To accomplish this release, a pitcher needs strong fingers and
wrist. Drills 15 and 16 are good wrist and finger strengtheners.

15. Finger Press

Objective — To strengthen the wrist and finger muscles.
Procedure — Slightly spread index finger and middle finger of the
pitching hand. Press both fingers into the palm of the
opposite hand. Push down hard for 5 seconds, then
release. Repeat 15 to 20 times.

Time — 1½ to 3 minutes.

Some shot-putters use a stationary forearm exercise to strength-
en their wrists and improve their release snap. It works like this: A
partner holds the shot-putter's forearm in an upright position while
the athlete releases with his fingers.

16. Shot-put Release

Objective — To develop a strong snap release.
Procedure — Gather 3 or 4 baseballs and a measuring tape. Pick
up a ball with the pitching hand. With the opposite
hand, grab forearm and hold it in an upright position,
parallel with the body. (Figure 12.) Flip the ball forward. Repeat several times. Measure each toss.
Comment — Repeat exercise often. Suggestion: Work Drill 15 prior
to Drill 16. Record all measurements on the Snap Release Chart.

The follow-through completes the pitching motion. After the
hurler releases the ball, his entire body shifts forward. The pitching

(FIGURE 12)

Snap Release Chart	
Date	
Toss Number	Distance (feet)
1	
2	
3	
4	
5	
6	
7	

arm whips forward and down. Both feet are nearly parallel with body weight slightly forward over the feet. The pitcher should be ready to field any ball hit his way.

Study your pitchers carefully and alert catchers to watch for these mistakes hurlers frequently make:

- Pitcher slows down or nearly stops body motion after releasing the ball.
- Pitcher fails to carry arm forward and down after releasing the ball.
- Pitcher fails to keep body weight evenly distributed over his feet. He pulls to the left or to the right after releasing the ball.
- Pitcher fails to stride forward, i.e., he does not point his lead foot toward home after releasing the ball.
- Pitcher fails to release ball with a strong wrist snap.

The next 4 drills require the pitcher to make a complete follow-through and to come quickly off the mound.

17. Straddling the Line

Objective — To practice making a complete follow-through.
Procedure — With a stick, draw a long line perpendicular to the pitcher's mound. Practice the pitching motion with no ball. Alternate throwing from a wind up and stretch position. After completing the delivery, reach for the ground with the pitching hand and bring the glove hand in front of the body. Concentrate on planting the left foot on the left side of the line and the right foot on the right side of the line. Keep body weight evenly distributed over both feet. (Figure 13.)
Comment — Advise pitchers to work this drill at home. Suggestion: Have pitchers lay 3 or 4 rocks on the perpendicular line ahead of the mound. Tell them to pick up the rocks, one at a time, after each delivery.
Time — 5 minutes.

18. Shot Back

Objective — To practice making a complete follow-through.
Procedure — Pitchers and catchers pair off and stand about 60 feet apart. With a stick, draw a long line perpendicular to

(FIGURE 13)

the pitcher's mound. After the pitcher makes his delivery, the catcher fires the ball back at him. The hurler must be ready to stop balls coming his way. Repeat several times.

Comment — Remind pitchers to keep their eyes on the catcher's target and hold their gloves in front of their bodies. Have the catchers alternate throwing balls to the left, to the right, and in front of the pitchers.

Time — 10 to 15 minutes.

19. Base Toss

Objective — To practice coming off the mound.

Procedure — Four pitchers go to the diamond and position themselves according to Figure 14. Player 1 scatters 3 baseballs approximately 30 to 40 feet apart between the mound and home plate. Player 2 stands at first base, Player 3 goes to third base, and Player 4 stays near home plate.

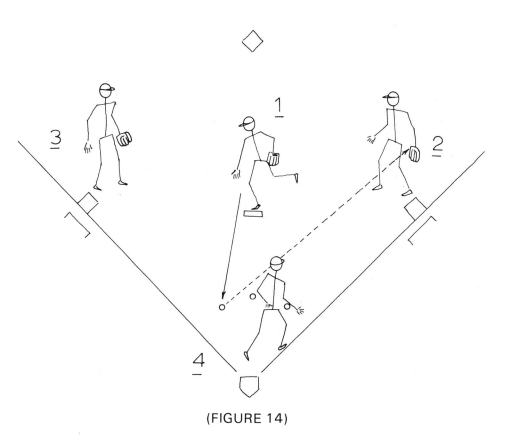

(FIGURE 14)

Action begins when Player 1, pitcher, winds up (without a ball) and simulates throwing a pitch to home plate. After the delivery, he races toward a ball, fields it, and throws to first base. He returns to the mound, repeats the same procedure, and throws a ball to Player 3 and Player 4. The basemen return balls behind the pitcher's mound. Athletes rotate in order. Player 1 becomes Player 2, Player 2 becomes Player 3, and so forth. Have each athlete field and throw 9 to 12 balls.

Comment — Have pitchers fire off the mound, field quickly, and make accurate throws. Remind basemen to give a clear target. Caution pitchers to space balls far enough apart to prevent stepping on them.

Time — 20 minutes.

20. Opposite Direction

Objective — To practice coming off the mound.
Procedure — Four pitchers go to the diamond and position themselves according to Figure 15. Player 1 sets 3 baseballs on the first base line, and 3 baseballs on the third
base line. Player 2 goes to first base, Player 3 stands
behind the pitcher's mound, and Player 4 goes to third
base.

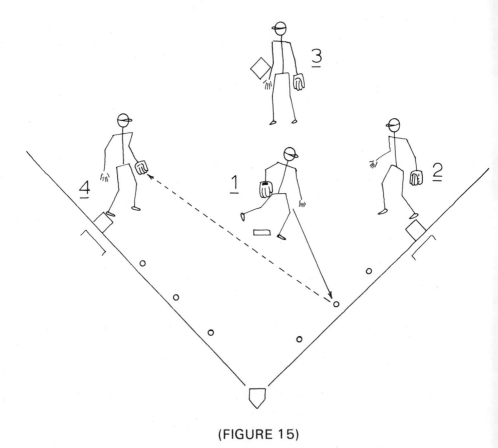

(FIGURE 15)

Action begins when Player 1, pitcher, winds up
(without a ball) and simulates throwing a pitch to
home plate. After the delivery, he runs toward the
first base line, fields each ball in turn, and throws to
third base. The baseman tosses the balls to Player 3.

Player 1 returns to the mound, simulates a pitch to home plate, runs toward the third base line, fields each ball in turn, and throws to first base. The baseman tosses the balls to Player 3. Athletes rotate in order. Player 1 becomes Player 2, Player 2 becomes Player 3, and so forth. Have each athlete field and throw 12 balls.

Comment — See Drill 19: Base Toss
Time — 20 minutes.

It's been said that a pitcher with a lightning fast ball and a curve that suddenly drops isn't worth beans unless he can throw strikes. One of the greatest assets a pitcher can have is control or the ability to move the ball around the strike zone.

We've seen how the warm-up session helps to prepare muscles for running and throwing. Some pitchers develop control problems when they hurry through their warm-ups and fail to loosen up properly. A coach can help overcome these difficulties by posting a daily schedule that includes a time slot for exercises and activities for the day's program.

The following chart shows a sample early season practice session:

5 minutes	20 minutes	30-35 minutes	20 minutes	25 minutes
Jogging around the field.	Stretching and bending exercises.	Pitchers pair off and throw. Warm up slow and work on control. (15 min.) Pitchers and catchers pair off. Work on Drill 14, Drill 18, Drill 19, or Drill 20. (15-20 min.)	Work on fielding bunts, covering first base, etc.	Pitchers pair off and do pick-ups. (10 min.) Work on wind sprints the last few minutes of practice. (15 min.)

Early Season Practice

Pitchers try different methods for sharpening their control. Here are some popular techniques:

- The pitcher ties string (cord line) between 2 wooden poles in order to set up a target over home plate. He adjusts the string to cover the strike zone. A catcher, wearing protective equipment, goes to home plate. The pitcher throws balls to different spots within the target area.
- The hurler tapes or draws a strike zone against a wall. He throws a tennis ball or soft rubber ball at the target. Note: Some coaches do not want their pitchers to throw tennis balls. A smart pitcher who warms his arm properly, throws at half speed and doesn't try to break off curve balls, should not strain his arm.
- The catcher moves his mitt around home plate giving the pitcher different targets. The hurler pitches to one spot until he can throw strikes consistently. The catcher then moves his target to a new area.
- A batter stands at home plate. He models different styles of hitting, e.g., open stance, closed stance, crouching at the plate, and so on. The pitcher and catcher combine strategy and work on the hitter's weakness. For example, if the catcher sees the hitter using a closed stance, he holds his glove on the low, inside corner of home plate. Note: The batter does not swing at the pitch.

The remaining 4 drills help a pitcher sharpen his control.

21. Wild High

Objective — To help the pitcher keep the ball low in the strike zone.

Procedure — Pitchers and catchers pair off and stand about 60 feet apart. Hurlers work on throwing low strikes. Note: There are times a pitcher has trouble keeping the ball low. When this happens, have the pitcher and catcher make these adjustments:
- Tell the hurler to bring his pitching arm down more before releasing the ball.
- Advise the catcher to hold his mitt around the batter's knees. Tell the catcher to show his whole

glove to the pitcher, not tilt it down toward the ground. Suggestion: If the pitcher continues to throw high, have him follow-through and touch the ground with his pitching hand (See Drill 17). Watch that he keeps his eyes on the target.

- Sometimes the hurler needs to shift his feet to the left or to the right of the pitcher's mound. Try to keep adjustments simple. Too many changes may throw off a pitcher's timing.

Time — 15 to 20 minutes.

22. Wild Low

Objective — To help the pitcher bring the ball up in the strike zone.

Procedure — Pitchers and catchers pair off and stand about 60 feet apart. Hurlers work on throwing high strikes. Note: When a pitcher has trouble bringing the ball up, have the pitcher and catcher make these adjustments:

- Tell the hurler to release the ball sooner.
- Advise the catcher to hold his mitt high in the strike zone, i.e., around the batter's belt buckle.

Comment — A high pitch can be dangerous when a strong hitter comes to the plate. However, when a hurler finds it tough to throw strikes, it's often better to take a chance than to let runners advance on wild pitches and walks.

Time — 15 to 20 minutes.

23. Low Ball Game

Objective — To keep the ball low in the strike zone.

Procedure — Pitchers pair off, stand about 60 feet apart, and take turns pitching and catching. Each hurler throws half an inning or 3 outs. The object is to throw knee high pitches on the inside corner and the outside corner of home plate. Use a rubber base for home plate. Here are the game rules:

- A strike is any pitch that hits the low inside corner or low outside corner of home plate.
- A ball is any pitch that misses the target area.

- The pitcher throws to a hypothetical batter. Whenever he walks a batter, a run is charged against him. The pitching catcher calls balls and strikes.
- The game lasts 3 innings (optional). The athlete giving up the least number of runs wins the contest.

Comment — Tell pitchers to watch the target and follow-through completely. Have pitchers throw at one half to three-quarter speed.

Time — 20 to 25 minutes.

24. Guide Hand

Objective — To practice throwing strikes.

Procedure — Pitchers and catchers pair off and stand about 60 feet apart. The catcher moves his mitt around the strike zone. The pitcher concentrates on bringing his guide hand (pitching hand) around and releasing the ball at the right moment. The right moment is when the pitcher can see his guide hand through the corner of his eye. The right moment release along with the complete follow-through helps a pitcher hit the target.

Comment — It takes constant practice and adjustments in the pitching motion to find the right moment to release the ball. The catcher is in excellent position to help the pitcher.

Time — 15 to 20 minutes.

These final points help pitchers find success throughout the season:

- Study the daily posted schedule. Know what to do and when to do it. If questions arise, check with the coach.
- Get into shape gradually. Don't be in a hurry to throw hard or break-off curve balls before arm muscles are ready.
- Remember that control doesn't come easy. It requires steady concentration and hard work to move the ball around the strike zone.
- Alternate throwing from a stretch and wind-up position. Many hurlers fail to work long enough on pitching from the stretch position.
- To be effective, a pitcher needs a repertoire of pitches. He

can't rely on throwing the same pitch to every batter. He must work with the catcher to spot a batter's weakness, then adjust his pitches accordingly.

- Keep the ball low in the strike zone. A batter can only see part of the ball when he's looking down on it.
- Be in good physical condition before the first practice. Include bending and stretching exercises, running, and throwing in the pre-practice workouts.
- Warm up properly during cool weather. Protect pitching arm at all times.

Utilizing Early Season Exercises and Drills for All Players

A good conditioning program includes stretching, strengthening, and running activities for every athlete on the squad. Many of the drills and exercises presented here can be extended throughout the season.

25. Five-Phase Exercise

Objective — To have athletes warm up prior to daily practice and games.

Procedure — *Phase 1* — Jog 2 laps around the baseball field or run the bases 5 times. Keep players running close together.

Phase 2 — Lie flat on back with arms pressed against the ground. Hold legs together. (Figure 16 A.) Slowly draw legs toward head. (Figure 16B.) Return to resting position. Repeat 5 times.

Phase 3 — Sit on ground with legs spread in hurdler's position. Keep hands together and point them toward the lead foot. (Figure 17A.) Lower head until you can touch the lead knee with your forehead. (Figure 17B.)

Return to resting position. Repeat 5 times. Exchange positions, i.e., use the opposite leg as the lead foot. Continue exercise and touch forehead to this knee. Return to resting position. Repeat 5 times.

Phase 4 — Athletes pair off. Partner A holds his hands together behind his neck. He tries to lift his hands upward while Partner B, standing behind him, holds them down. (Figure 18.) Partner B waits 5 seconds, then releases his grip. Repeat 5 times. Athletes switch positions and continue exercise.

(FIGURE 16A.)

(FIGURE 16B.)

(FIGURE 17A.)

(FIGURE 17B.)

(FIGURE 18)

Phase 5 — Place back against screen. Extend arms over head, grab the screen, and slowly lower body until arms support body weight. (Figure 19.) Hang for 5 seconds. Return to resting position. Repeat 5 times.

(FIGURE 19)

Comment — Begin this exercise after the team begins to get into shape. Have players take turns leading the exercise.

26. Sprint the Circle

Objective — To strengthen the legs.

Procedure — Break the team into 4 groups. Send each group to a different area on the field. Have each group do the following:
  • Make a 5-foot circle on the ground. Use lime, cord line, or anything that will show the boundary of the circle.

- Place 4 baseballs about 30 feet away from the circle. (Figure 20.) Players form a line about 10 feet from Ball One.

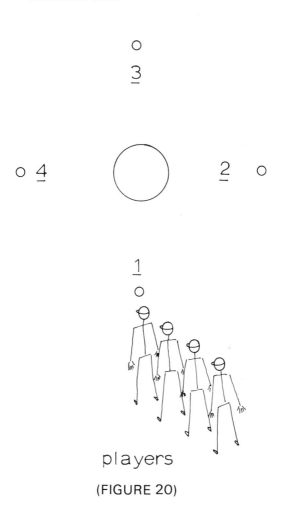

(FIGURE 20)

- Action begins when the first player in line runs to Ball One, picks it up, sprints to the circle, and drops the ball inside of the circle. *Rule:* Ball must remain inside of the circle; if it rolls out, the athlete must return and replace the ball. The player continues to pick up each ball, in turn, and drop it inside the circle. He returns to the line and tags the

next runner. The next athlete sprints to the circle
and replaces each ball.
- Each player sprints to the circle 4 times.

Comment — Spice up the drill by having athletes time each other
with a stop watch. The competitive factor adds ex-
citement to the activity. *Suggestion:* After each athlete sprints to the circle two times, move the balls 40
feet away from the circle.

Time — 15 to 20 minutes.

27. Twenty Minute Warm-Up for Outfielders

Objective — To properly warm-up the throwing arm.

Procedure — Outfielders pair off and stand about 50 feet apart.
They play catch for approximately 5 minutes, then
gradually move back until they are about 150 feet
apart. Suggestion: Have players make chest high
throws to the glove side of their partners. Urge athletes to hold the ball with a cross-seam grip (See Drill
12: *Grip Toss)*. Outfielders should throw hard the last
5 minutes. Hard throwing readies arm muscles for
making long, difficult throws.

Comment — Stress the importance of making correct throws.
Some athletes believe the warm-up session is a time
to throw curves, knuckle balls, and other pitches that
have no value to the outfielder. Remind athletes that
arm strain may result from throwing too hard and for
too long a time.

Time — 20 minutes.

28. Twenty Minute Warm-Up for Infielders

Objective — To properly warm-up the throwing arm and practice
fielding ground balls.

Procedure — Infielders pair off and stand about 50 feet apart. They
play catch for approximately 5 minutes, then gradually
move back until they are about 90 feet apart. Suggestion: Have players make chest high throws to the glove
side of their partners. Urge athletes to hold the ball
with a cross-seam grip (See Drill 12: *Grip Toss*). Tell

infielders to alternate throwing overhand, three-quarters, and sidearm. Have them roll ground balls to the left and to the right of each other for the last 4 or 5 minutes.

Comment — If possible, let the infielders (and outfielders) warm-up the same way each day.

Time — 20 minutes.

29. Infield Around

Objective — To practice making throws around the infield.

Procedure — Infielders, excluding pitcher, take their positions. Catcher brings a baseball to home plate. The ball travels around the infield 5 times, or 5 rounds, in this manner:

Round 1 — Catcher -- Third -- Shortstop -- Second -- First -- Catcher.

Round 2 — Catcher -- First -- Second -- Shortstop -- Third -- Catcher.

Round 3 — Catcher -- Second -- Third -- First -- Short-stop -- Catcher.

Round 4 — Catcher -- Shortstop -- First -- Third -- Second -- Catcher.

Round 5 — Catcher tosses a ground ball to the third baseman. The baseman fields and throws the ball home. The catcher repeats toss-ing a ground ball, in turn, to the short-stop, second baseman, and first baseman.

Comment — Play *Infield Around* before hitting regular infield. Remind athletes to make chest high throws to the glove side of the base.

Time — 5 minutes.

30. Outfield Around

Objective — To practice throwing and fielding the ball.

Procedure — Outfielders take their positions. If more than 3 players participate, use extra baseballs. The left fielder starts action by throwing a ball chest high to the glove side of the center fielder. He, in turn, makes a chest high throw to the right fielder. The right fielder tosses the ball back to the center fielder who returns it to the left fielder. Each athlete throws and fields the ball two times.

The second round follows the same pattern, but requires each athlete to make a single-bounce throw to one another. Each outfielder throws and fields the ball two times.

Comment — Have outfielders field and throw while the infielders are playing *Infield Around.* Remind outfielders to make an overhand throw with a complete follow-through. If time permits, have outfielders mix throwing single bouncers with high, pop flies.

Time — 5 minutes.

The following 10 drills help build up wind while strengthening the leg and arm muscles:

31. Fade Away

Objective — To practice running, fielding, and throwing.

Procedure — Players bring their gloves and form 2 parallel lines about 50 feet apart. The coach and back-up man (team manager) stand between the 2 lines. (Figure 21.)

When the coach yells "Go," the first player in each line runs straight ahead. The coach hollers "Now," and throws a baseball over the players' heads. Both players chase the ball. The athlete closest to the ball fields it, and the player farthest away drops back and takes the throw. He, in turn, pivots and throws the ball to the back-up man. Returning players go to opposite lines. Each athlete fields and throws 3 or 4 times.

Time — 15 to 20 minutes.

32. In and Out

Objective — To practice running the bases, fielding, and throwing.

Procedure — Players bring their gloves and line up near home plate. The coach and back-up man (team manager) stand at home plate. (Figure 22.)

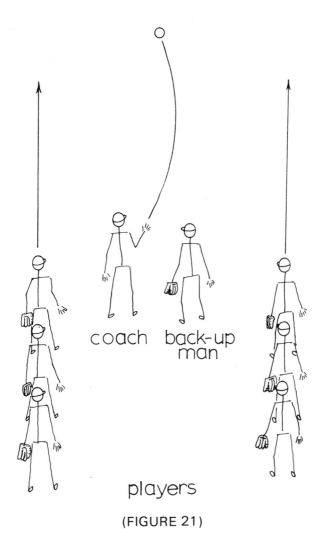

coach back-up
man

players

(FIGURE 21)

When the coach yells "Go," the first player in line runs toward first base, rounds it, and heads for second base. After touching second base, the runner dashes toward center field. The coach hits a long fly ball to the player. The athlete fields and throws to the back-up man. After throwing the ball, he immediately sprints toward home plate. The back-up man rolls the ball to the pitcher's mound. The player fields and makes an underhand flip to the back-up man, and returns to the end of the line.

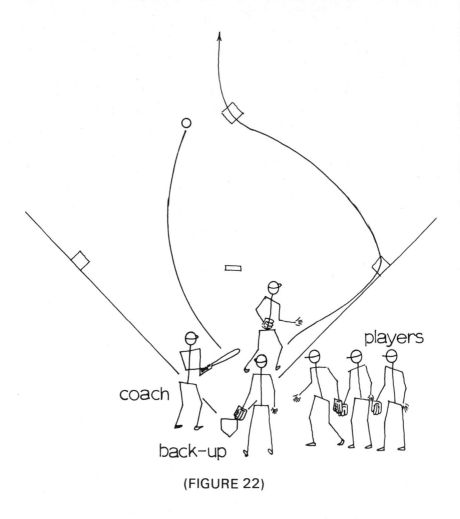

(FIGURE 22)

Comment — Before starting the drill, show athletes the proper way to run down the base line and round first base. Suggestion: Divide team into 2 separate groups of 9 or 10 players. Athletes can take turns backing-up and hitting the ball.

Time — 15 to 20 minutes.

33. Circle Four

Objective — To practice running the bases, fielding, and throwing.

Procedure — Players bring their gloves and line up near home plate. The coach and back-up man (team manager) stand at home plate.

When the coach yells "Go," the first player in line circles every base, steps on home plate, and heads back to first. He touches the bag and runs toward center field. The coach hits a long fly ball to the player. The athlete fields the ball and runs hard to home plate. He hands the ball to the back-up man and returns to the line. Athletes receive 3 or 4 chances to run and field.

Comment — Alternate Drill 32 with Drill 33. Have players run Drill 32 the first 2 rounds and Drill 33 the last 2 rounds.

Time — 20 minutes.

34. Double Shotgun

Objective — To practice running and fielding.

Procedure — Athletes bring their gloves and line up on the field. The coach and designated hitter bring a fungo bat and ball with them. A back-up man (manager) stands near the coach. (Figure 23.)

Action begins when the first player in line runs straight ahead at full speed. The coach hits a line drive to the left or to the right of the player. After the player fields and throws to the back-up man, the designated hitter fungos a short fly ball in front of the fielder. The back-up man moves near the designated hitter and takes the throw. The fielder sprints to the end of the line. Each athlete fields and throws 6 to 8 times.

Comment — Pitchers generally make good fungo hitters. Have them take turns fungoing the ball. Suggestion: Make the drill competitive. Award one point for every successful play. A bobbled ball or bad throw wipes out the score. The athlete earning the most points wins.

Time — 15 to 20 minutes.

35. Dead Ball Relay

Objective — To strengthen the legs.

Procedure — Players form 4 lines on the field with 4 or 5 athletes

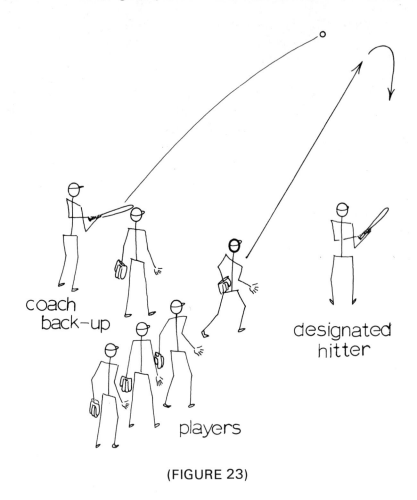

coach
back-up

designated
hitter

players

(FIGURE 23)

per line. (Figure 24.) Keep lines about 180 feet apart. Make a 12-inch circle between opposite lines with cord line or lime. Place a baseball inside of each circle.

On command "Go," Player 1 from Lines 1 and 3 sprint to the ball, pick it up, run to Player 1 of Lines 2 and 4, hand him the ball, and go to the end of their line. Player 1 from Lines 2 and 4, running at full speed, replace the ball in the circle, tag Player 2 in Lines 1 and 3, and go to the end of the line. Action continues until every athlete runs 4 times. Repeat drill for 2 or 3 rounds.

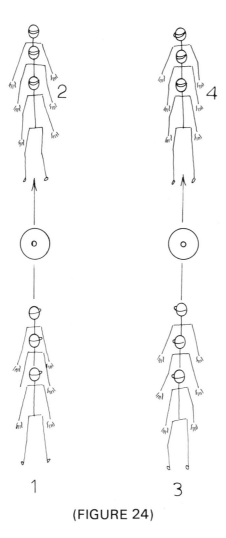

(FIGURE 24)

Comment — Set up a competitive relay. After each round, have the losing athletes do 10 push-ups. Try to keep the same number of players in each line. If the ball rolls out of the circle, the erring team automatically loses the round.

Time — 10 to 15 minutes.

36. Glove-Bat Relay

Objective — To strengthen the legs.

Procedure — Players form 4 lines on the field with 4 or 5 athletes per line. Keep lines about 30 feet apart. Place a glove holding a ball approximately 90 feet ahead of each line and a bat another 90 feet beyond the glove. (Figure 25.)

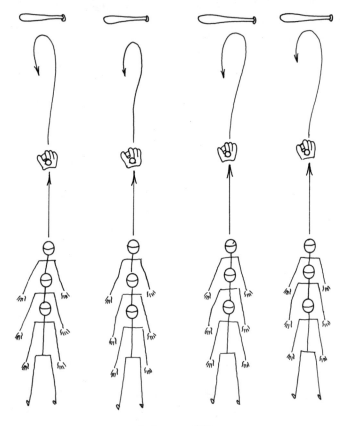

(FIGURE 25)

On command "Go," the first athlete in each line sprints to the glove, picks up the ball, runs to the bat, and sets the ball next to the fat end of the bat. He races back to the line and touches Player 2. Player 2 runs to the bat, picks up the ball, sprints to the glove and replaces the ball in the glove. He races back to the line and touches Player 3. The cycle continues with each athlete running 2 times per round.

Comment — Set up a 2-round relay. Repeat 3 or 4 times. Have the losing team do 10 push-ups. Try to keep the same number of players in each line.

Time — 15 to 20 minutes.

37. Boomerang Relay

Objective — To practice fielding and running.

Procedure — Players bring their gloves and form 3 lines on the field. Make a 12-inch circle with cord line or lime about 60 feet ahead of each line. Place a ball in each circle. A player stands approximately 200 feet ahead of his line. He acts as tosser. (Figure 26.)

On command "Go," the first athlete in line charges the ball, picks it up with both hands, and throws to the tosser. He then sprints around the tosser, and heads back to the line. The tosser yells "Catch," and throws a looping fly ball to the athlete. The player fields the ball, replaces it in the circle, and tags the next person in line. Each player runs the course 2 times or 1 round. After 1 round, the tosser goes to the end of the line. Athletes take turns running, fielding, and throwing.

Comment — Make the losing team members do 10 push-ups after each round. If a player misplays the toss or picks up the placed ball with one hand, his team automatically loses the round.

Time — 20 minutes.

38. Field-A-Thon

Objective — To practice fielding and throwing.

Procedure — Players bring their gloves to the field. Four players, tossers, form a line and stand about 50 feet apart. Each tosser holds a ball. The remaining athletes form a vertical line to the right of the tossers. Player 1 stands approximately 100 feet to the right of his line. (Figure 27.)

On command "Go," Player 1 breaks to his left. He fields and returns the balls thrown by each tosser.

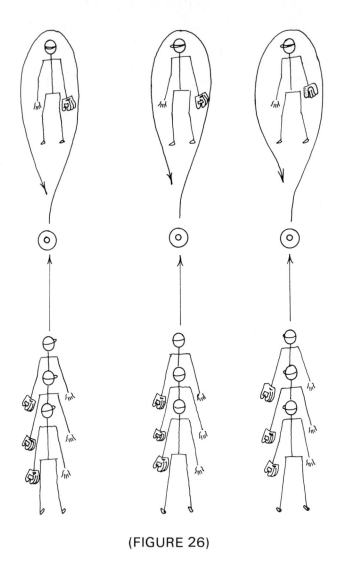

(FIGURE 26)

For example, Tosser 1 rolls a slow bouncing ball to Player 1. Player 1 fields and throws the ball back to Tosser 1. Action continues as Tosser 2 delivers a long fly ball, Tosser 3 throws a single bouncer, and Tosser 4 delivers a high bouncing ball. Player 1 returns to the line. Each athlete runs the course 3 times before changing positions with the tossers.

Comment — Two groups of 8 to 10 players can work this drill at

(FIGURE 27)

the same time. Keep groups far enough apart to prevent collisions.

Time — 20 to 25 minutes.

39. Hat Relay

Objective — To strengthen the legs.

Procedure — Players form 3 lines on the field. Keep lines approximately 30 to 40 feet apart. Place a baseball about 90 feet in front of each line. (Figure 28.)

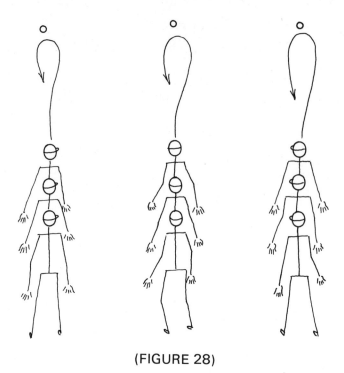

(FIGURE 28)

On command "Go," the first player in each line
runs full speed at the ball, drops his hat over the ball,
turns and runs back to his starting position. When he
reaches the starting point, he turns and runs to his
hat, picks it up, sprints back to the line, and tags the
next runner. All players run the course 2 times.

Comment — The runner cannot return to the line until his hat
completely covers the ball. Try to keep the same number of athletes in each line. Each line should have its
share of fast runners. Have the losing team members
do 10 push-ups. Continue action as long as time permits.

Time — 20 minutes.

40. Triple Hat Drop Relay

Objective — To strengthen the legs.

Procedure — Players form 3 lines on the field. Keep lines approximately 30 to 40 feet apart. Place 3 baseballs approxi-

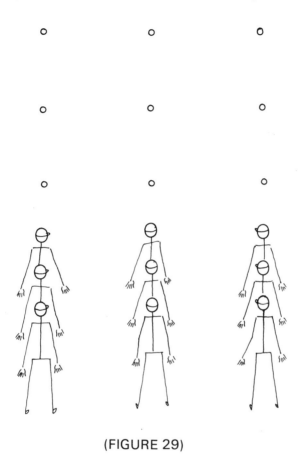

(FIGURE 29)

mately 40 feet apart in the front of each line. (Figure 29.)

On command "Go," the first player in each line runs at full speed to Ball 1, drops his hat over it, turns and runs back to his starting position. When he reaches the starting point, he turns and runs to his hat, picks it up, sprints to Ball 2, drops his hat over it, turns and runs back to his starting position. He repeats the same procedure for Ball 3. After the player drops his hat over Ball 3, he immediately picks up his hat, races back to the line, and tags the next athlete. All players run the course 2 times.

Comment — See Comment for Drill 39: *Hat Relay.*
Time — 20 minutes.

How to Use Conditioning Activities in Practice

A wise coach will spend the first few weeks on conditioning exercises and drills. He'll give his athletes plenty of running, throwing, stretching and bending exercises for the arms, legs, shoulders, back and trunk.

Now let's see how these activities fit into a 3-week practice schedule. Keep in mind these plans are only suggestions. How you organize a team depends upon available time, number of players, type of facilities, game schedule, and coaching philosophy.

First Week:

Have pitchers pair off and work Drill 12 (Chapter 1) during the warm-up period (the warm-up period follows the exercise block on the chart) for the first 3 days. Assign Drills 18, 19, 20 or 24 (Chapter 1) the last 2 days of the week. Give pitchers pick-up drills and wind sprints the last 25 minutes of practice. Urge hurlers to include Drills 8, 9, 10 and 11 (Chapter 1) in the workout.

Second Week:

Have pitchers work all week with catchers during the warm-up period (the warm-up period follows the exercise block on the chart). Assign Drills 14, 16, 18 or 24 from Chapter 1.

On Tuesday and Thursday, let pitchers hit balls to the outfielders during infield practice. They can take turns fielding, hitting, and backing-up throws.

On Wednesday and Friday, have pitchers and catchers work batting practice. Pitchers should throw at half speed while concentrating on tossing strikes. Tell catchers to practice on footwork and blocking wild pitches. If possible, hold 2-station batting practice. For example, divide the players into 2 groups. Have one group hit from the left side of the batting cage, and the other group hit from the right side of the batting cage. Assign pitchers pick-ups and wind sprints the last 25 minutes of practice.

Give players a variety of pepper drills. Pepper games offering points keep athletes interested and encourages hard play.

Scheduling problems arise during early season practice. Some athletes may be competing in basketball or wrestling tournaments. Infield and outfield practice may have to be postponed until a later time. If that's the case, fill the time period with conditioning drills.

First Week (Approximate practice time: 2 hours)

Day	5 min.	15-20 min.	20 min.	15-20 min.	20-25 min.	25 min.
Monday	Jog	Exercise	Drills 27 and 28	Drill 35	Drill 33	Drill 39
Tuesday	Jog	Exercise	Drills 27 and 28	Drill 37	Drill 38	Wind sprint relays
Wednesday	Jog	Exercise	Drills 27 and 28	Drill 31	Drill 34	Drill 40
Thursday	Jog	Exercise	Drills 27 and 28	Drill 36	Drill 32	Wind sprint relays
Friday	Jog	Exercise	Drills 27 and 28	Drill 26	Drill 31	Drill 40

Three Week Practice Schedule — First Week

Second Week (Approximate practice time: 2 hours, 20 min.)

Day	5 min.	15-20 min.	20 min.	20 min.	20-25 min.	20-25 min.	25 min.
Monday	Jog	Exercise	Drills 27 and 28	Pepper	Drills 31, 32 or 33	Drills 34, 35, 36 37	Wind sprint relays
Tuesday	Jog	Exercise	Drills 27 and 28	Pepper	Drills 32, 33 or 36. Do Drills 29 and 30 before taking infield and and outfield.		Drill 39
Wednesday	Jog	Exercise	Drills 27 and 28	Pepper	Batting Practice		Drill 40
Thursday	Jog	Exercise	Drills 27 and 28	Pepper	Drills 32, 33 or 36. Do Drills 29 and 30 before taking infield and outfield.		Wind sprint relays
Friday	Jog	Exercise	Drills 27 and 28	Pepper	Batting Practice		Drill 40

Three Week Practice Schedule — Second Week

Third Week (Approximate practice time: 2 hours, 25 min.)

Day	5 min.	10-15 min.	20 min.	20 min.	50-60 min.	25 min.
Monday	Jog	Exercise	Drills 27 and 28	Drill 31	Batting practice	Drill 39
Tuesday	Jog	Exercise	Drills 27 and 28	Pepper	Work on bunting. Do Drills 29 and 30 before taking inf./outfield	Wind sprint relays
Wednesday	Jog	Exercise	Drills 27 and 28	Intra-squad Game		Drill 40
Thursday	Jog	Exercise	Drills 27 and 28	Pepper	Work on base running. Do Drills 29 & 30 before taking inf./outfield	Wind sprint relays
Friday	Jog	Exercise	Drills 27 and 28	Intra-squad Game		Wind sprint relays

Three Week Practice Schedule — Third Week

Third Week:

On Monday, assign pitchers and catchers batting practice. Have pitchers throw three-quarter speed and mix fast balls with off-speed pitches. If pitchers have trouble keeping the curve ball in the strike zone, tell them to throw straight balls.

On Tuesday and Thursday, let pitchers hit balls to the outfield during infield practice. They can take turns fielding, hitting, and backing-up throws.

Have pitchers and extra athletes who are not playing in the intra-squad game work on pepper, bunting, or fielding drills. Pitchers about to enter the game should warm up along the side lines.

The Value of Team Drills

Athletes benefit from team drills in these ways:

- Players keep busy. Everyone knows what to do and what is expected of him.
- These activities give athletes plenty of running, fielding, and throwing.
- Many drills provide a competitive atmosphere by allowing players to earn points for accurate throws and clean fielding.
- The coach can walk around and observe his players. He's in an excellent position to offer help to erring athletes.

3

Employing Fast-Moving Drills
for Small Groups

One of the biggest problems a coach faces is how to keep every player busy during practice. We've found that small groups of athletes (3 to 6 players), spread out over the field, can work on several skills at the same time. For example, Drill 55: *Bungo,* requires a team to split into 3 or 4 five-man units. Each unit practices bunting, base running, and sliding. Small group activities also reduce the monotony of daily practice.

The following suggestions will help your practice run smoothly:
- Introduce one drill at a time.
- Make sure athletes understand what is expected of them.
- Start and stop activities on time.

Drills For Three Players

41. Infielder Go and Throw

Objective — To practice fielding, throwing, and tagging the base.
Procedure — Three infielders go to an open area on the field and bring a ball, rubber base, and gloves with them. They position themselves according to Figure 30. Player 1 stands 90 feet ahead of the base; Player 2 stays 90 feet to the left of the base; Player 3 stands 90 feet to the

69

right of the base. Player 1 sets a baseball between himself and the base.

Action begins when Player 1, moving at full speed, fields the ball, throws it to Player 2, and continues running until he reaches the base. Player 2 relays to Player 3, and Player 3 makes a low throw to the glove side of Player 1. Player 1 tags the base and returns to his starting position. He replaces the ball on his way back. Player 1 runs the course again only this time he throws to Player 3. After 2 runs, athletes rotate clockwise. Player 1 becomes Player 2, Player 2 becomes Player 3, and so on.

Comment — Let infielders repeat the drill several times. Tell athletes to field quickly and make accurate throws.

Time — 15 to 20 minutes.

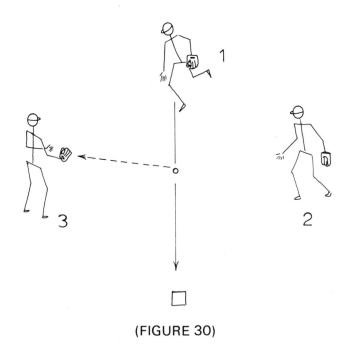

(FIGURE 30)

42. Outfielder Go and Throw

Objective — To practice fielding and throwing.

Procedure — Three outfielders bring their gloves and a baseball to an open area on the field. They stand about 100 feet apart. (Figure 31.)

Action begins when Player 3 throws a ball to the right of Player 1. After the throw, Player 3 breaks to a point about 50 feet in front of Player 2. He acts as cut-off man for Player 2. Player 1 fields and throws the ball chest high to the glove side of Player 3. If the throw is off target, Player 2 yells "Cut," and Player 3 catches the ball, turns, and throws it to Player 2. If the ball is on target, Player 2 yells "Go," and Player 3 moves out of the way. Action continues as Player 2 throws a ball to the left of Player 1. After the throw, Player 2 becomes cut-off man, and Player 3 takes the throw. After 2 chances, athletes rotate clockwise. Player 1 becomes Player 2, Player 2 becomes Player 3, and so on.

Comment — Have athletes mix tossing long fly balls, single bouncers, and ground balls.

Time — 15 to 20 minutes.

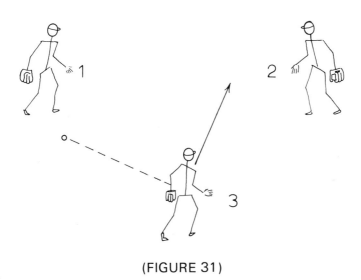

(FIGURE 31)

43. Poke

Objective — To practice hitting the ball.

Procedure — Three players bring their gloves, a bat, and a ball near a side line fence. Player 1, hitter, stands near the fence. Player 2, pitcher, stands about 60 feet in front of Player 1. Player 3, fielder, stays approximately 100 feet behind Player 2. Player 1 receives 5 swings. He tries to poke or punch the ball between the pitcher and fielder.

Play *Poke* for points. Each time an athlete hits the ball between the pitcher and fielder, award one point. The athlete earning the most points wins. After the batter takes 5 swings, players rotate. Player 1 becomes Player 3, etc.

Comment — Tell athletes to watch the ball carefully and concentrate on driving the pitch up the middle.

Time — 20 minutes.

44. Triangle

Objective — To practice fielding and throwing.

Procedure — Three players bring their gloves and a ball to an open area on the field. They stand about 100 feet apart and form a triangle.

Player 1, tosses the ball, calls out "Two" or "Three." If he says "Two," Player 2 fields and throws to Player 3. Player 3 relays to Player 1. The tosser should see that Player 2 and Player 3 field the same number of balls. After each athlete fields and throws 4 or 5 times, players rotate clockwise.

Comment — Tell Player 1 to mix throwing ground balls, pop flies, single bouncers, or long fly balls. Have him make the fielders hustle, but not to the point of exhaustion.

Time — 15 to 20 minutes.

45. Hit Split

Objective — To practice fielding and throwing.

Procedure — Three players bring their gloves, a bat, and a ball to an open area on the field. Athletes stand about 100 feet apart and form a triangle.

Player 1, batter, fungos a ball to the right of Player 2. Player 3 moves to a point about 50 feet in front of Player 1. Player 2 makes a chest high throw to the glove side of Player 3. Player 2 turns and runs toward Player 1. Player 3 tosses a looping ball just over the head of Player 2. Player 2 fields, throws to Player 1, and returns to his position. Action continues when Player 3 fields the ball and follows the same procedure. Each athlete fields 2 times before rotating clockwise.

Time — 15 to 20 minutes.

46. Bunt the Lines

Objective — To practice bunting the ball.

Procedure — Three players bring their gloves, a bat, and 2 balls near a side line fence. Player 1, bunter, stays near the fence. Players 2 and 3, fielders, stand about 20 feet apart and approximately 90 feet in front of Player 1.

Players 2 and 3 hold a baseball and take turns pitching to Player 1. When Player 2 throws, the hitter bunts the ball to the left side of the field. Player 2 fields the ball and returns to his position. When Player 3 throws, the hitter bunts the ball to the right side of the field. Player 3 fields the ball and returns to his position. Each athlete bunts the ball 6 times before rotating clockwise. Player 1 becomes Player 2, Player 2 becomes Player 3, etc.

Time — 20 minutes.

Drills For Four Players

47. Three Seconds

Objective — To practice fielding and throwing.

Procedure — Four players bring their gloves to an open area on the field. Players 1, 2, and 3 form a line and stay about 20 feet apart. They stand approximately 100 feet in front of the coach. Player 4, back-up man, stands about 20 feet to the right of the coach. (Figure 32.)

Action begins when the coach hits 3 balls 3 seconds apart, to Players 1, 2, and 3, in turn. Player 4 then positions himself about 30 feet in front of the coach. Fielders throw the ball to Player 4. Player 4 returns the balls to the coach. Each athlete fields 5 balls before rotating clockwise. Player 1 becomes Player 2, Player 2 becomes Player 3, and so on.

Comment — Timing is very important. The coach must place his hits so the back-up man receives only one throw at a time.

Time — 20 minutes.

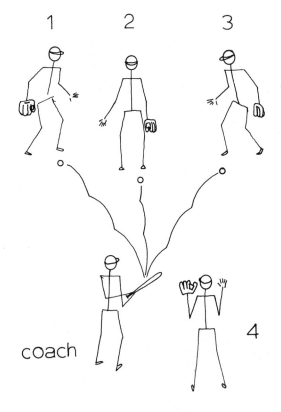

(FIGURE 32)

48. I Pattern

Objective — To practice fielding and throwing.

Procedure — Four players bring their gloves to an open area on the field. Players 1, 2, and 3 form a line and stay about 50 feet apart. Player 3 stands approximately 150 feet in front of the coach (he is the farthest away). Player 4, back-up man, remains about 20 feet to the right of the coach. (Figure 33.)

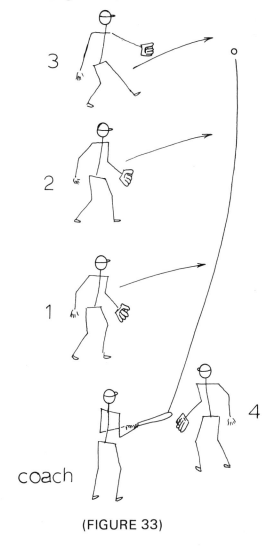

3

2

1

4

coach

(FIGURE 33)

Action begins when the coach hits a deep fly ball to Player 1. Players 2 and 3 line up between Players 1 and 4. Player 4 hollers directions to Players 2 and 3. For example, he either yells out "To the right"

or "To the left." Player 1 fields and throws to Player
2. Player 2 relays to Player 3, and Player 3 fires the ball
to Player 4. Each athlete fields 2 times before rotating.
Player 3 becomes Player 4, Player 4 becomes Player
1, Player 1 becomes Player 2, and Player 2 becomes
Player 3.

Time — 20 minutes.

49. I Pattern Shift

Objective — To practice fielding and throwing.
Procedure — The procedure is the same as Drill 48: *I Pattern,* with
one exception: Player 1 fields 3 balls before rotating.
The coach hits the first ball to the left of Player 1,
the second ball to his right, and the third ball over
his head.
Comment — This activity requires athletes to run harder and make
longer throws.
Time — 20 minutes.

50. Pepper Punch*

Objective — To practice hitting, fielding, and throwing.
Procedure — Four players bring their gloves, a bat, a ball, and a
rubber base near a side line fence. Player 3, pitcher,
stands approximately 60 feet away from home plate.
Player 2, fielder, stays 30 to 40 feet to the left of Player 3. Player 4, fielder, stands 30 to 40 feet to the right
of Player 3. Player 1, batter, comes to home plate
(rubber base).

Player 1 receives 6 swings. If he hits the ball to
Player 2, Player 2 fields and throws to Player 4. Player
4 relays to Player 3. If he hits the ball to Player 4,
Player 4 fields and throws to Player 2. Player 2 relays
to Player 3. If he hits the ball to Player 3, Player 3
throws to either Player 2 or Player 4. After 6 swings,
athletes rotate clockwise.

*Hoehn, Robert G., *Baseball Drills For Small Groups,* (Thomas J. Rowen Booklet
Service: Santa Clara, CA., 1975) pp. 8-10.

Comment — Tell athletes to keep throws chest high and to the glove side. Remind them to stay in a low fielding position, glove near the ground, and field baseballs out in front of their bodies.

Here's a suggestion: Whenever you run a pepper drill, have fielders stay 60 feet away from the batter. This allows the batter to adjust his swing and time the ball properly. Make sure athletes throw from one-half to three-quarters speed.

This activity gives infielders excellent practice in charging slow bouncing balls and making tough sidearm throws.

Time — 20 to 25 minutes.

51. Six Rounds

Objective — To strengthen the legs and practice running the bases.

Procedure — Four players go to an open area on the field and set up a miniature diamond by placing 4 rubber bases approximately 60 feet apart. A baseball rests between first and second base. Athletes line up near home base.

Action begins when Player 1 takes off from home, tags first, and heads for second. He picks up the ball and continues to round each base. He rounds the bases 6 times. The pattern looks like this:

ROUND	PROCEDURE
1	Round bases. Pick up ball between first and second base.
2	Round bases. Set ball between second and third base.
3	Round bases. Pick up ball between second and third base.
4	Round bases. Set ball between third and home plate.
5	Round bases. Pick up ball between third and home base.
6	Round bases. Set ball between first and second base.

Comment — *Six Rounds* is an excellent early season conditioning drill. Suggestion: Let athletes time each other
with a stop watch.

As players get into shape, work *Six Rounds* on
the baseball diamond. Prior to the drill, show athletes
the proper way to run the bases.

Time — 20 to 25 minutes.

Drills For Five Players

52. Firing Squad

Objective — To practice fielding and throwing.

Procedure — Five players bring their gloves, 3 bats, and 3 balls near
a side line fence. Players 1, 2 and 3, hitters, form a
line and stay about 20 feet apart. Player 5, fielder,
remains near the fence approximately 90 feet away
from the hitters. Player 4, back-up man, stays to the
left of the hitters. (Figure 34.)

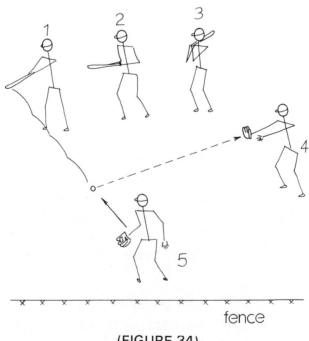

(FIGURE 34)

Action begins when the hitters, in turn, fungo a ground ball to the fielder. For example, Player 1 hits a ball to the fielder. The athlete fields and throws to the back-up man. Players 2 and 3 follow by fungoing a ground ball to the fielder. Player 5 receives 9 chances to field before athletes rotate. Player 1 becomes Player 2, Player 2 becomes Player 3, and so on.

Comment — Caution hitters to stay alert. Under no circumstances should 2 players hit a ball to a fielder at the same time.

Time — 20 minutes.

53. Four Point Game

Objective — To practice throwing, hitting, and fielding.

Procedure — Five players bring their gloves, a bat, and a ball near a side line fence. Player 1, pitcher, stands about 60 feet away from Player 2, hitter. Players 3, 4 and 5, fielders, spread out in the field. (Figure 35.) Player 2 receives 4 swings. He tries to hit the pitches as follows:

Pitch	Where to hit ball
1	Player 1, pitcher
2	Player 3, left side of field
3	Player 4, right side of field
4	Player 5, up the middle of field

Each time Player 2 places the ball correctly, he earns one point. The athlete with the most points wins. A swing and miss, pop up, or foul counts as one swing. After 4 swings, players rotate clockwise. Player 1 becomes Player 2, Player 2 becomes Player 3, and so on.

Comment — Have Player 1 throw one-half speed and concentrate on throwing strikes.

Time — 20 minutes.

54. Up and Down the Line

Objective — To practice throwing, hitting, and fielding.

Procedure — Players bring their gloves, bats, and a ball near a side

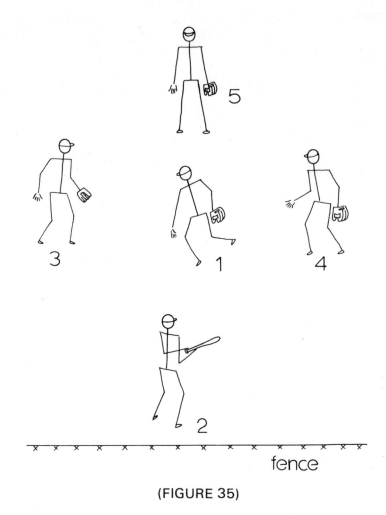

fence

(FIGURE 35)

line fence. Players 1, 2, 3 and 4, fielders, form a line and stay about 20 feet apart. Player 5, hitter, remains near the fence and stands approximately 60 feet from the fielders.

Action begins when Player 1 tosses the ball to Player 5. Player 5 must hit the ball to each fielder in succession. For example, he hits the throw from Player 1 to Player 2. He hits the throw from Player 2 to Player 3, and so on. He continues to bat until he misses, fouls, or hits the ball to the wrong player. When the batter fails to hit successfully, athletes rotate clockwise. Player 5 becomes Player 1, Player 1 becomes Player 2, and so forth.

Time — 20 minutes.

55. Bungo*

Objective — To practice throwing, fielding, hitting, bunting, sliding, and base running.

Procedure — Five players bring their gloves, bats, and a ball near a side line fence. They make a miniature baseball field with rubber bases spaced approximately 60 feet apart.

Athletes position themselves according to Figure 36.

Player 1 — Pitcher, throws one-half speed

Player 2 — Baseman, plays near second base

Player 3 — Fielder, plays left-center, medium deep

Player 4 — Fielder, plays center-right, medium deep

Player 5 — Batter

The batter receives 3 swings. He must: (1) bunt the first pitch down the third base line (batter stays at home plate); (2) bunt the second pitch down the first base line (batter stays at home plate); (3) hit the third pitch into the outfield, runs to first, rounds the base, and slides into second base. If the ball stays in the infield, the batter need only run to first.

Fielding players have the following responsibilities:

Player 1 — Concentrates on throwing strikes. Fields balls hit within his area; covers first base when Player 2 makes a play.

Player 2 — Fields balls hit to left, right, and over the second base bag; covers first base when Player 1 makes a play.

Player 3 — Fields balls hit between center field and the third base line.

Player 4 — Fields balls hit between center field and the first base line.

After 3 swings, athletes rotate clockwise. Pitcher comes to bat, batter goes to left-center, left-center

---

*Ibid, pp. 20-24.

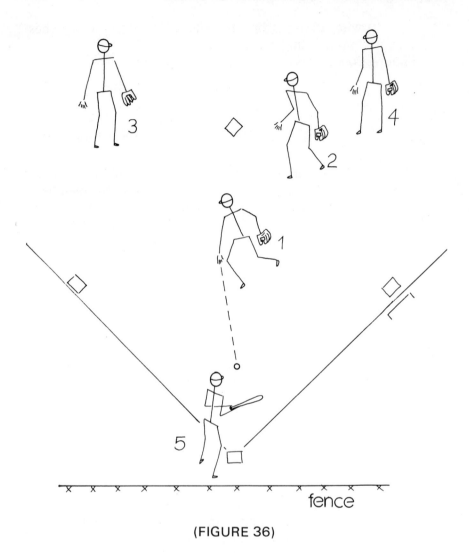

(FIGURE 36)

shifts to center-right, center-right moves to second base, and second baseman takes the mound.

Turn *Bungo* into a point game. Award points as follows:

1 Point — The batter reaches base on an error, bunts the ball into fair territory, or beats out an infield hit.

> 2 Points — Reaches second safely after hitting the third ball.
>
> 5 Points — Bunts the first and second ball into fair territory (down each base line); reaches second base safely.
>
> 0 Points — Balls hit over the outfielders heads, balls bunted foul, or batters thrown out at first or second base.

Comment — Players practice bunting balls down each base line, punching the ball between outfielders, running the bases, and sliding into second base. Give athletes pre-drill base running and sliding instructions. Make sure athletes wear sliding pads and pants covering their legs.

Time — 25 to 30 minutes.

Drills For Six Players

56. Move About Game

Objective — To practice place hitting and fielding.

Procedure — Six players bring their gloves, bats, and a ball near a side line fence. Athletes scatter around the field as shown in Figure 37. They stay far enough apart to allow fielding room. Player 1, hitter, stands by the fence. Player 4, pitcher, stays about 60 feet away from Player 1.

Player 1 receives 4 pitches. He must hit each ball in the following manner:

Pitch 1 — Bunt to Player 2, fielder

Pitch 2 — Place hit to Player 3, fielder

Pitch 3 — Place hit to Player 5, fielder

Pitch 4 — Bunt to Player 6, fielder

Set up game points. Award one point for every successful hit. The batter with the most points wins. After Player 1 hits, athletes rotate clockwise. Player 1 becomes Player 2, Player 2 becomes Player 3, and so forth.

Time — 20 to 25 minutes.

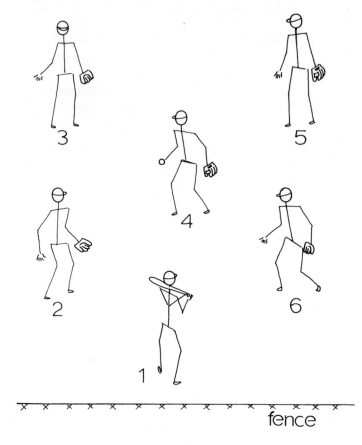

(FIGURE 37)

57. Drop and Pop

Objective — To practice bunting, hitting, and fielding.

Procedure — Six players bring their gloves, bats, and a ball near a side line fence. Athletes position themselves according to Figure 38. Player 1, hitter, stands near the fence. Players 2 and 3, fielders, stay close together about 40 feet to the left of Player 1. Players 5 and 6, fielders, stay close together about 40 feet to the right of Player 1. Player 4, pitcher, stands about 60 feet in front of Player 1.

     Action begins when Player 4 throws 4 pitches to

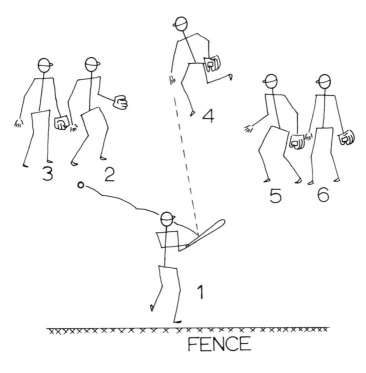

FENCE

(FIGURE 38)

Player 1. Player 1 bunts the first pitch to the left side of the field. Player 3 fields and throws to Player 4. After the throw, Player 2 breaks to his left. Player 1 hits the second pitch to Player 2. Action continues as Player 1 bunts a third pitch to Player 6. Player 6 fields and throws to Player 4. After the throw, Player 5 breaks to his right. Player 1 hits a fourth pitch to Player 5. After 4 pitches, athletes rotate clockwise. Player 1 becomes Player 2, Player 2 becomes Player 3, and so on.

Comment — Remind Player 4 not to throw the ball until Players 2 and 5 make their breaks. Turn *Drop and Pop* into a point game. Award one point for every successful hit. The athlete with the most points wins.

Time — 20 to 25 minutes.

58. Fungo Run Game*

Objective — To sharpen throwing, fielding, and base running skills.

Procedure — Six players bring rubber bases, gloves, bats, and balls to an open area on the field. They make a diamond with bases approximately 60 feet apart. Athletes position themselves in the following manner:

Player 1 — First hitter
Player 2 — Second hitter
Player 3 — Catcher
Player 4 — Left field, medium deep
Player 5 — Center field, medium deep
Player 6 — Right field, medium deep

Here are the game rules for *Fungo Run:*

- Player 1 comes to home plate, fungos a ball into the outfield, and runs the bases.
- The outfielders, working together, attempt to put out Player 1. For example, if Player 1 hits a ball into center field, the left fielder covers second or third base and tries to tag out Player 1.
- Player 2, second hitter, must fungo a ball that will score Player 1. If he fails, Player 1 is out and must return to home plate. Player 1 becomes the hitter and play continues.
- After 3 outs, athletes rotate. Player 1 becomes Player 2, Player 2 becomes Player 3, and so on.
- Athletes make outs when they: (1) fly out, pop out, or line out to a fielder (catcher included); (2) miss or foul the ball; (3) interfere with play, run out of the base line, etc.; (4) fail to touch a base; (5) hit the ball into the infield, i.e., slow ground ball; (6) hit the ball over an outfielder's head; (7) attempt to steal or slide; (8) leave the base before the batter hits the ball.

Each player keeps track of runs scored. The athlete scoring the most runs wins.

Time — 25 to 30 minutes.

Ibid., pp. 35-38.

59. Target Zone Game*

Objective — To practice hitting, fielding and throwing.
Procedure — Six players carry rubber bases, six old towels, gloves, bats, and balls near a side line fence. They make a diamond with bases approximately 60 feet apart. Athletes position themselves in the following manner:
Player 1 — Hitter
Player 2 — Pitcher, throws one-half speed
Player 3 — Rover, plays between the pitcher and out-field. The hitter can move the rover any-where he wishes.
Player 4 — Left field, medium deep
Player 5 — Center field, medium deep
Player 6 — Right field, medium deep

Two towels should be placed 15 to 20 feet apart in left field, center field, and right field. (Figure 39.)

Action begins when Player 1 comes to home plate. He receives 6 swings. He tries to hit the pitched ball into the target areas marked by the towels. Hitters earn points as follows:

3 points — Ball hits the target area, i.e., lands on the towels or between the towels. Fielders judge each hit. An outfielder cannot catch the ball before it hits the ground unless it travels beyond the target area.

2 points — Ball lands within 3 or 4 feet of the target.

1 point — A fielder bobbles the ball or plays the ball before it reaches the target area. A fielder can play a ground ball hit into the out-field without penalty.

0 points — Balls landing outside the target areas.

After 6 swings, athletes rotate. Player 1 becomes Player 2, Player 2 becomes Player 3, and so on. The athlete earning the most points after 2 rounds wins.

Comment — Tell hitters to try to punch the ball over the rover's head into the target area. If a player (right-hander) wishes to hit inside pitches into left field, he tells the

*Ibid., pp. 38-40.

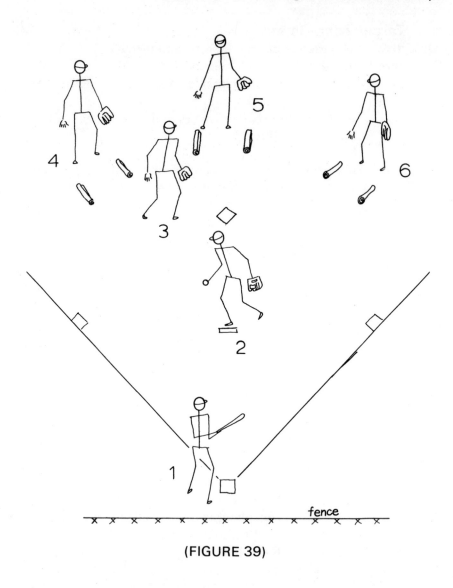

(FIGURE 39)

pitcher to keep balls on the inside corner of home plate. He may also wave the rover toward the third base line.

A smart hitter will choke the bat, swing easy, and hit the ball where it's pitched.

Time — 25 to 30 minutes.

4

Activities to Help Infielders Improve Their Fielding and Throwing

An athlete doesn't become a good infielder overnight. He has to work hard, very hard, to perfect the skills necessary for successful team play.

Prior to infield drills, review the following points:

- Keep body low by bending at the knees. Lower buttocks and touch glove to the ground.
- Bring body weight forward, up over balls of feet. Keep feet comfortably spread with the left foot slightly forward of the right foot.
- Stay balanced. Be ready to move quickly to the left, to the right, or straight ahead.
- Fix eyes on the ball. Keep arms extended forward, palms turned inward, and fingers held together.
- After ball rolls into glove, trap it by bringing the throwing hand over ball. Draw glove to body, and bring arm back to throwing position.
- Release ball with a complete follow-through motion. Step toward the direction of the throw.

60. Stay Low and Throw

Objective — To practice fielding and throwing.

Procedure — Infielders go to the diamond. They split into 2 lines, A and B. Group A forms a line near third base; Group B gathers near first base. The coach and back-up man (manager or pitcher) come to home plate. (Figure 40.)

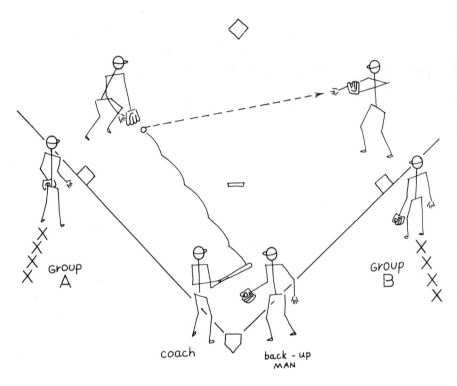

(FIGURE 40)

Action begins when a Group A player takes a low fielding position to the left of third base. *Note:* Remind athlete to bend at the knees, keep body weight forward, and touch his glove to the ground. The coach rolls a slow bouncing ball to the fielder. When the coach yells "Field," the player charges, scoops up the ball, and makes a throw to first base. A Group B player takes the throw. He returns the ball to the back-up man. After making the throw, Player A goes to Line B; Player B goes to Line A.

Comment — Let each athlete field and throw several times. Tell players to keep their weight forward and extend arms toward the ball. This helps bring the body in a low fielding position.

Time — 10 to 15 minutes.

61. Fielding Three

Objective — To practice fielding and throwing.

Procedure — Infielders go to the diamond. They split into 2 groups, A and B. Group A forms a line near third base; Group B gathers near first base. The coach and back-up man (manager or pitcher) come to home plate. The back-up man places 2 baseballs on the diamond. He sets the first ball about 20 feet in front of third base and the second ball about 20 feet in front of second base. (Figure 41.)

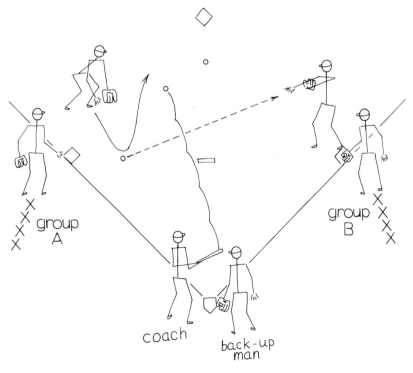

group A   group B

coach   back-up man

(FIGURE 41)

Action begins when a Group A player takes a low fielding position to the left of third base. A Group B player goes to first base. When the coach yells "Go," the Player A fields the first ball and makes a throw to first base. He immediately turns to his left and breaks toward shortstop. The coach hits a ground ball to the player's left. The athlete fields and throws to first base. After the throw, he picks up the second placed ball and throws to first base. The back-up man replaces each ball. Player A goes to Line B; Player B goes to Line A.

Comment — Remind athletes to keep low and touch their gloves to the ground. Let each player field and throw 2 or 3 rounds.

Time — 15 to 20 minutes.

62. High Hop

Objective — To practice fielding and throwing.

Procedure — Infielders line up near third base. The coach and back-up man (manager or pitcher) come to home plate. The first player in line assumes a low fielding position to the left of third base.

Action begins when the coach hits a high bouncing ball to the left of the player. He fields and throws to the back-up man. The coach hits another high bouncer to the player's right. He fields and throws to the back-up man. The player goes to the end of the line.

Comment — When fielding balls that bounce above the belt, tell athletes to keep thumbs together, point fingers upward, and turn palms toward the ball.

Time — 10 to 15 minutes.

63. Straight Ahead

Objective — To practice fielding and throwing.

Procedure — Infielders line up near shortstop. The coach and back-up man (manager or pitcher) come to home plate. The first player in line assumes a low fielding position.

Action begins when the coach hits a hard ground ball directly at the player. The player fields and throws the ball to the back-up man. He returns to the end of the line. Each athlete fields and throws 5 or 6 times.

Comment — Remind fielders to stay low, charge the ball, and keep their bodies in front of the ball. Watch for these faults: (1) The athlete lets the ball play him, i.e., waits too long to field the ball; (2) he hurries the throw; (3) he turns his body to one side while fielding.

Time — 10 to 15 minutes.

64. Side To Side

Objective — To practice fielding and throwing.

Procedure — Infielders line up about 20 feet in front of second base. The coach and back-up man (manager or pitcher) come to home plate. The first player in line takes a low fielding position.

Action begins when the coach hits a ball to the left of the fielder. The athlete fields, throws to the back-up man, and returns to a fielding position. The coach hits a ball to the right of the fielder. The athlete fields, throws to the back-up man, and goes to the end of the line.

Comment — On balls hit to the left, have players stay low, shift to that side, and get to the ball quickly. On balls hit to the right, have players stay low, shift to that side, get to the ball quickly, plant right foot hard in the ground, and throw.

How a player fields depends on ball speed. For example, the faster the ball travels, the quicker an athlete must react. *Suggestion:* Mix hitting hard, medium, and slow ground balls.

Time — 15 to 20 minutes.

65. Triple Pick

Objective — To practice fielding and throwing.

Procedure — Infielders bring their gloves to an open area on the field. They place 3 baseballs approximately 90 to 100 feet apart to form a triangle. Player 1, first athlete in line, becomes the fielder. Player 2, second athlete in line, becomes the back-up man. He stands about 60 feet to the right of the line. (Figure 42.)

Action begins when the back-up man calls "Right," "Left," or "Front." If he yells "Left," the fielder breaks left, scoops up the placed ball, and throws to the back-up man. After the throw, the back-up man calls out "Right" or "Front." The player fields and throws. The back-up man replaces each ball. Both fielder and back-up man return to the line.

Comment — Let each athlete field and catch the ball 3 or 4 times. Remind athletes to stay low and be ready to break in any direction.

Time — 15 minutes.

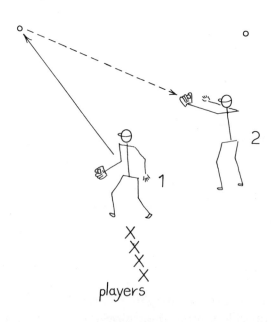

players

(FIGURE 42)

66. Combo Fielding Game

Objective — To practice fielding and throwing.

Procedure — Infielders line up near shortstop. The coach, back-up man (manager or pitcher), and runners come to home plate. The coach hits 4 balls, one at a time, to the left, to the right, or directly at the fielder. The athlete, assuming a low fielding position, must be ready for anything hit his way.

Action begins when the coach hits a ball to the first fielder in line. A runner breaks for first base. (Figure 43.) He continues running the bases until he reaches home plate. The player fields and throws each ball to the back-up man.

Award points in the following manner:

1 point — Player fields cleanly and makes a good throw to the back-up man.

2 points — The last throw beats the runner to home plate.

If a player makes an error, he loses all of his points. The coach judges every play.

Each athlete fields and throws 4 times before going to the end of the line. Optional: The game consists of 2 rounds or 8 chances to field and throw. An athlete, playing 2 rounds, can score up to 10 points.

Comment — Make sure runners wear protective equipment. Do not let runners slide into home plate. Advise the back-up man to stay behind home plate and not to attempt to tag out the runner.

Time — 20 minutes.

67. Slow-Hit

Objective — To practice fielding and throwing.

Procedure — Infielders, including pitcher and catcher, go to their positions. The coach and runners line up near home plate. *Suggestion:* Let extra players run the bases until they enter the drill.

Action begins when the pitcher throws a ball to the catcher. A runner breaks for first when the ball hits the catcher's glove. Then, the coach alternates

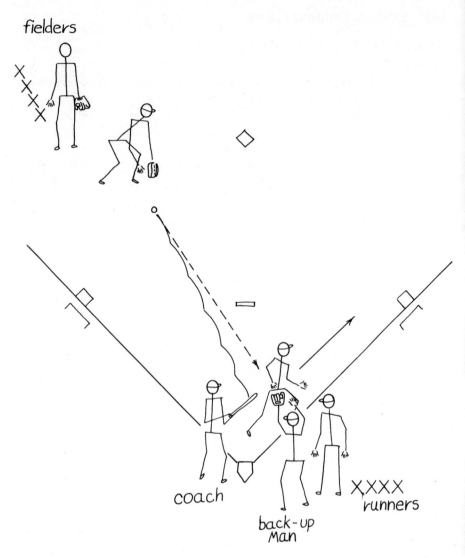

(FIGURE 43)

hitting a high, slow bouncing ball between third base and shortstop or between second base and first base. Infielders play the ball and back up bases accordingly. Runners stay on base until they make an out.

Comment — Slow-hit balls between infielders create problems. For example, a ball bouncing slowly toward shortstop or second base allows the runner to get a good jump. The third baseman and first baseman should make every effort to cut off slow bouncers and throw out the runner.

Occasionally hit a high bouncer over the pitcher's head. This gives the shortstop practice in coming across the diamond.

Time — 15 minutes.

68. Single Runner Around

Objective — To practice fielding and throwing.

Procedure — Infielders, including pitcher and catcher, go to their positions. The coach and runners line up near home plate. *Suggestion:* Let extra players run the bases until they enter the drill.

Action begins when the pitcher throws a ball to the catcher. When the ball reaches the catcher's mitt, a runner breaks for first, and the coach fungos a ball to an infielder. The fielder must stop the runner from reaching base. If he succeeds, the runner returns to the line. If he fails, the runner goes to second base. Here are the rules for *Single Runner Around:*

- A runner is safe on an error or late throw.
- If a runner beats a throw to first, he is awarded second base.
- The lead runner may advance only one base at a time. For example, a runner on second or third or runners at second and third advance to the next base if the runner going to first beats the throw or is safe on an error. If the runner makes an out, players clear the bases and return to the line.
- A runner on third scores when the runner going to first reaches base safely.
- Runners advance one base on overthrows.
- The fielder tries to get the runner at first. He *does not* throw to any other base.
- After 3 outs, runners clear the bases.
- When a runner scores, all infielders do 5 push-ups.

Comment — The success of the drill hinges on the coach's ability to place his hits. A ball that forces the fielder to run hard and throw quickly keeps the play close.

Time — 25 to 30 minutes.

69. Batter's Choice

Objective — To practice fielding and throwing.

Procedure — Infielders, including pitcher and catcher, go to their positions. Five players, batters, line up near home plate. *Note:* Use good hitting athletes for batters. Advise hitters to choke the bat, i.e., move hands up on the handle and concentrate on spraying the ball around the infield.

Batters have 4 choices: (1) a sacrifice bunt; (2) drag bunt for a base hit; (3) push bunt for a base hit; (4) hit a ground ball, pop fly, or soft line drive.

Action begins when a batter comes to home plate. The pitcher, hurling at half speed, throws to the catcher. The batter receives 2 swings or 2 chances to hit the ball. He runs out balls hit into fair territory. When the hitter makes an out, he returns to the line and bats in order. *Note:* A batter is automatically out if he hits a ball over an infielder's head. After 3 outs, runners return to the line, and bat in order.

Comment — Advise pitchers to throw straight balls down the middle of home plate. Have them throw from the stretch with men on base. Allow runners to slide. Be sure the catcher, hitters, and runners wear protective equipment.

This activity offers excellent practice in bunt defense, base running, and backing-up the bases. The coach can stop play and make corrections at any time.

Time — 20 to 25 minutes.

70. Third or Bust

Objective — To practice fielding and throwing.

Procedure — Infielders, including pitcher and catcher, go to their positions. The coach comes to home plate. Runners line up near first base. *Suggestion:* Let extra players run until they enter the drill.

Action begins when a runner goes to first base. The pitcher delivers the ball to the catcher. When the pitch reaches the catcher's mitt, the runner breaks for second and the coach fungos a slow roller, high bouncer, or bunt onto the infield. The runner, moving at full speed, rounds second and heads for third. The fielder attempts to throw the runner out at third base. *Note:* The third baseman or shortstop must tag out the runner. If the third baseman fields the ball, the shortstop covers the bag. If the fielder tags out the runner, the runner returns to the line. When a runner beats the throw, he goes to the line, and all infielders do 5 push-ups. Play continues with another runner going to first.

Comment — Infielders work on bunt defense and backing-up bases. Allow runners to slide. Make sure the catcher and runners wear protective equipment. *Note:* When the third baseman fields a bunt down the line, have the catcher cover third and the pitcher cover home plate.

Time — 15 minutes.

71. On the Go

Objective — To practice fielding and throwing.

Procedure — Infielders, excluding pitcher, go to their positions. The coach brings a fungo bat to home plate.

Action begins when the coach hits 4 balls, one at a time, to each player. For example, he hits 4 balls to the third baseman, 4 balls to the shortstop, and so on. The chart on the following page shows where the coach hits each ball and where players throw the ball:

Comment — Go 4 rounds. Keep the first 2 rounds moving at a slow pace. This will give athletes a chance to learn the procedure. The activity taxes a player's ability to concentrate, react quickly, and make good throws.

Player	Ball	Where coach hits ball	Where players throw ball (numbers indicate player positions)
Third baseman	1	Toward second. Baseman fields and stays at second.	Third baseman to 3; 3 to 2
	2	Down first base line. Baseman stays at first.	Third baseman to 4; 4 to 2
	3	Toward second. Baseman stays at second.	Third baseman to 3; 3 to 2
	4	To the left of third base.	5 to 3; 3 to 2
Shortstop	1	Toward second. Shortstop stays at second.	Shortstop to 3; 3 to 2
	2	Down first base line. Shortstop stays at first.	Shortstop to 4; 4 to 2
	3	Toward second. Shortstop stays at second.	Shortstop to 5; 5 to 2
	4	To the left of third base.	6 to 2
Second baseman	1	Toward first base. Baseman stays at first.	Second baseman to 6 covering second; 6 to 2
	2	Toward second. Baseman stays at second.	Second baseman to 3; 3 to 2
	3	Toward third base. Baseman stays at third.	Second baseman to 6 covering second; 6 to 2
	4	Toward second.	4 to 2
First baseman	1	Toward second. Baseman stays at second.	First baseman to 4 covering first; 4 to 2
	2	Toward third base. Baseman stays at third.	First baseman to 4; 4 to 2
	3	Toward second. Baseman stays at second.	First baseman to 5; 5 to 2
	4	Toward first base.	3 to 2

On the Go

Suggestion: Mix hitting hard ground balls with high, slow bounding balls.

Time — 20 to 25 minutes.

72. Get 'Em

Objective — To practice fielding and throwing.

Procedure — Infielders, including pitchers, form a line behind shortstop. A player, pitcher or extra catcher, goes to third base. Runners line up near first base. The coach and catcher come to home plate. A runner goes to first base. (Figure 44.)

Action begins when the coach hits a slow ground ball or high chopper toward right field. The runner breaks for second. He rounds second and heads for third. A player fields and throws to third. After the play, both runner and fielder return to their respective lines. Every athlete fields and throws twice.

The next runner in line comes to second base. Infielders move into shallow right field. Play continues when the coach hits a slow ground ball or high bouncer toward left field. The runner, breaking for third, attempts to reach home. A player fields and throws to home plate. After the play, both runner and fielder return to their respective lines. Every athlete fields and throws twice.

Comment — Keep the competitive atmosphere strong. Have the fielding athlete do 5 push-ups when the runner beats the throw.

Show catchers the proper way to tag out runners at home plate. Make sure the catcher and runners wear protective equipment. Allow runners to slide.

Time — 20 minutes.

73. Double Throw

Objective — To practice fielding and throwing.

Procedure — Infielders, including pitcher, go to their positions. The coach and runners stay near home plate.

Action begins when a runner comes to home

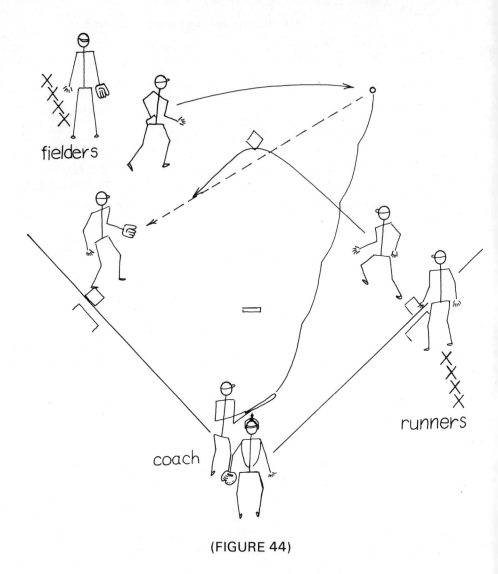

fielders

runners

coach

(FIGURE 44)

plate. The coach hits 2 hard ground balls to the third baseman. A runner breaks for first as soon as the baseman fields the ball. *Note:* Do not allow runners to leave early from home plate. The coach hits a second ball when the third baseman throws to first. The third baseman must field and throw quickly to get the runner. After each catch, the first baseman throws the ball to the catcher.

Play continues as the coach hits 2 balls, in turn, to the shortstop, second baseman, first baseman, and pitcher. Fielders back-up plays accordingly.

Comment — The coach must time his second hit to make a close play at first. Make sure runners wear protective helmets.

Time — 15 to 20 minutes.

74. One Base

Objective — To practice fielding and throwing.

Procedure — Infielders, excluding pitcher, go to their positions. The coach and runners stay near home plate.

Action begins when a runner comes to home plate. He takes off as the coach hits a ground ball to the third baseman. The baseman fields and throws to first. A runner, whether safe or out, stays on first. *Note:* The procedure remains the same for each base.

Play continues when the coach hits a ground ball, in turn, to the shortstop, second baseman, and first baseman. The runner advances one base each time the coach hits the ball. The first baseman, last player to field the ball, tries to throw the runner out at home plate. Each infielder throws the ball to the catcher.

Comment — Athletes, to be successful, must field and throw accurately. They must know ahead of time which base to cover.

Allow runners to slide into home plate. Be sure the catcher and runners wear protective equipment.

Time — 20 minutes.

75. Three Ball Haul

Objective — To practice fielding and throwing.

Procedure — Infielders, excluding pitcher, go to their positions. Runners line up near first base. The coach brings a fungo bat to home plate.

Action begins when a runner comes to first base. The coach hits 3 balls, one at a time, to the same fielder. For example, he hits 3 balls to the first baseman before hitting to another baseman. The runner goes from first base to second on the first hit, second to third on the second hit, and tags up from third on the last hit. *Note:* The runner, whether safe or out, stays on base. After touching home plate, the runner goes to the end of the line. Play continues as another runner goes to first.

The following chart shows where the coach hits each ball and where players throw the ball:

Player	Ball	Where coach hits ball	Where players throw ball (numbers indicate player positions)
First baseman	1	Down first base line	To 6 covering second; 6 to 2
	2	Toward second base	To 5; 5 to 2
	3	Fly to shallow right field	Runner tags up; 3 to 2
Second baseman	1	To the left of second base	To 6 covering second; 6 to 2
	2	Over second base bag	To 5; 5 to 2
	3	Fly to shallow center field	Runner tags up; 4 to 2
Shortstop	1	To the right of shortstop	To 4 covering second; 4 to 2
	2	Over second base bag	To 5; 5 to 2
	3	Fly to shallow center field	Runner tags up; 6 to 2
Third baseman	1	Down third base line	To 4 covering second; 4 to 2
	2	To the left of third base	To 6 covering third; 6 to 2
	3	Fly down the line in shallow left field	Runner tags up; 5 to 2

Three Ball Haul

Comment — Make the activity last 4 rounds. Move at a slow pace until athletes become familiar with the routine. Allow runners to slide. Be sure runners and catcher wear protective equipment.

Time — 20 to 25 minutes.

76. Going Home

Objective — To practice fielding and throwing.

Procedure — Infielders and runners gather near third base. The coach and catcher come to home plate. A runner goes to third base; a fielder positions himself between third base and shortstop. (Figure 45.)

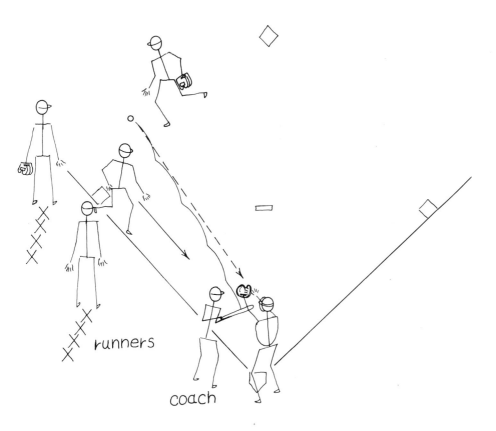

runners

coach

(FIGURE 45)

Action begins when the coach fungos a ground ball to the fielder. The runner breaks for home at the crack of the bat. The fielder throws to the catcher. The catcher steps on home plate. He makes no attempt to tag out the runner. The runner goes to the line and the fielder stays near second base.

Play continues when another runner goes to third base. The coach fungos a second ball to the left of second base. The runner breaks for home at the crack of the bat. The fielder throws to the catcher. The catcher must tag out the runner. The runner and fielder return to their respective lines. Let each athlete field and throw 6 to 8 times.

Comment — Have fielders keep throws low to the inside of home plate. A low throw is easier for a catcher to handle. A high throw pulls the catcher out of position and opens him to possible injury from a sliding runner. Make sure the catcher and runners wear protective equipment.

Time — 15 to 20 minutes.

5

Activities to Help Outfielders Improve Their Fielding and Throwing

An outfielder has an important job to do. He often runs a long way to make a catch. He may handle the ball only three or four times a game, but a leaping catch or a long throw may well determine the outcome of the contest.

An outfielder, to be successful, should show:

- The ability to make accurate overhand throws.
- Fair to good speed. He must be able to move quickly to his left, to his right, straight back, or directly ahead.
- Excellent hustle. He should be ready to back up the bases and sprint on and off the field.
- Baseball savvy. An alert outfielder studies each batter's stance and swing. He positions himself accordingly. He keeps his head in the game, looks for the cut-off man, and throws to the correct base.

The following 12 drills give an outfielder practice in judging fly balls and making accurate throws.

77. Break Left, Break Right

Objective — To practice getting a good jump on the ball.

Procedure — Outfielders go to the field and stand about 20 feet apart. The coach, acting as pitcher, simulates throwing a ball from either a stretch or wind up. The coach yells "Set," as he begins his pitching motion. After he completes his delivery, he calls out "Break left" or "Break right." (Figure 46.) He repeats the procedure several times.

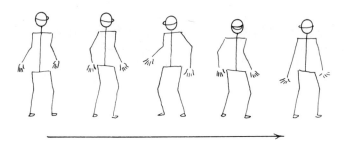

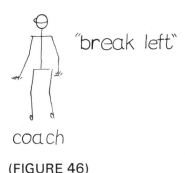

"break left"

coach

(FIGURE 46)

Comment — Go over these points with your outfielders:
- Bend at the knees; spread feet comfortably apart.
- Keep body weight forward over balls of feet.
- Extend arms forward out in front of body.
- Keep eyes glued on pitcher.

Break Left
- Swing body to left side; pivot on left foot.
- Throw right foot across left foot.
- Move toward ball. Watch the ball every moment.

Break Right
- Swing body to right side; pivot on right foot.
- Throw left foot across right foot.
- Move toward ball. Watch the ball every moment.

    Note: Watch players closely! Some outfielders stay back on their heels and fail to shift quickly to the side.

Time — 5 minutes.

78. Two and One

Objective — To practice fielding and throwing.
Procedure — Outfielders go to the field. A player, relay man, positions himself between the outfielders and coach. A back-up man, manager or pitcher, stands to the right of the coach. (Figure 47.)

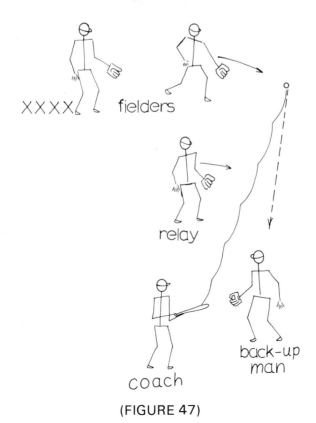

(FIGURE 47)

Action begins when the coach fungos 3 balls, one at a time, to the first outfielder in line. The following chart shows the hitting, fielding, and throwing pattern:

Ball	Where coach hits ball	Where fielder throws ball
1	Ground ball to fielder's right	To the back-up man
2	Ground ball to fielder's left	To the back-up man
3	High fly to fielder	To the relay man

On the third hit, the relay man drops into cut-off position by running toward the back-up man. The back-up man tells the relay man how to line up, i.e., to the left or to the right. The fielders makes a shoulder high overhand throw to the glove side of the relay man. After the play, the fielder becomes relay man, and relay man goes to the end of the fielder's line.

Comment — Have athletes field and throw several times. Stress the importance of making good throws to the relay man.

Time — 20 minutes.

79. Testing the Throwing Arm

Objective — To find strong throwing arms.

Procedure — Infielders take their positions. Outfielders line up in right field. Runners (extra players) gather near first base and the coach comes to home plate. (Figure 48.)

Action begins when a runner goes to first base. The coach fungos a base hit to right field. The first player in line fields and throws to third base. *Note:* Tell the runner to sprint full speed to third. After the play, the runner goes to the end of the line. Give outfielders several chances to throw the ball.

Comment — The man on first, base hit to right situation occurs frequently. It takes a strong arm to cut the runner down at third. This drill helps the coach to find a strong throwing right fielder.

The second baseman stays near the bag. Since

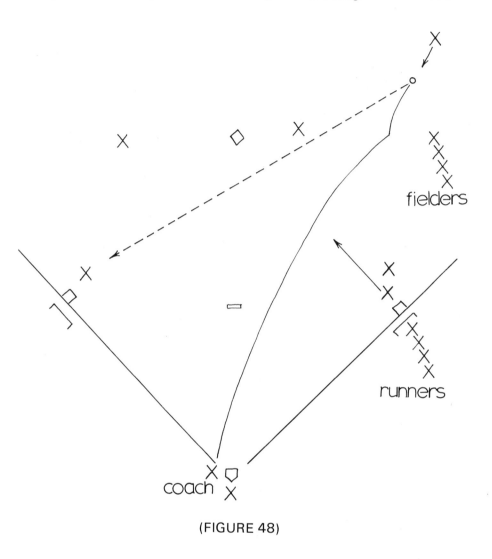

(FIGURE 48)

the outfielder throws to third, the second baseman doesn't have to enter short right field to become a relay man. If the ball gets by the outfielder, the baseman runs into right field and takes the relay. The shortstop covers second base. The shortstop acts as cut-off man for the outfielder. The third baseman tells the shortstop how to line up. The pitcher backs up third base.

Time — 15 to 20 minutes.

80. Three High

Objective — To practice fielding and throwing.
Procedure — Outfielders go to the field and line up about 200 feet away from the coach. Player 1, cut-off man, stays approximately 200 feet to the right of the coach. Player 2, back-up man, stands next to the coach. (Figure 49.)

Play begins when the coach hits 3 high flies, one at a time, to the fielder. He hits the first ball to the fielder's left, second ball directly in front of the fielder, and third ball to the player's right. The cut-off man positions himself in front of the back-up man to receive each throw. The back-up man tells the cut-off

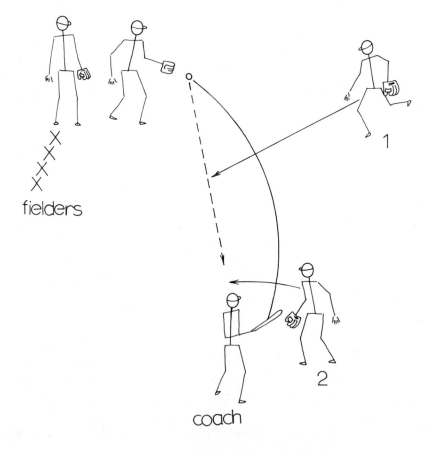

fielders

1

2

coach

(FIGURE 49)

man how to line up, i.e., to the left or to the right. The fielder makes a single bounce throw to the cut-off man.

Players rotate. Fielder becomes cut-off man, cut-off man becomes back-up man, and back-up man goes to the end of the fielding line. Repeat procedure several times.

Comment — Urge athletes to make hard overhand, single bounce throws to the cut-off man. A player must run hard, field cleanly, and make accurate throws.

Time — 20 minutes.

81. Three in Line

Objective — To practice fielding and throwing.

Procedure — Infielders go to their positions. Outfielders line up in left field and the coach stands near home plate. The shortstop sets 3 balls in a line about 20 feet apart and approximately 100 feet behind second base. Runners (extra players) line up at home plate. (Figure 50.)

Action begins when a runner comes to home plate. When the coach yells "Go," the runner takes off and the first fielder in line sprints toward Ball 1. He picks it up and makes a play on the runner. If the fielder throws out the runner, the runner returns to the end of the line. If the runner is safe, he stays on base. The fielder returns to his starting position and repeats the same procedure for Ball 2 and Ball 3.

The athlete fields all 3 balls, one at a time, before going to the line. The pitcher collects returning balls, throws them to the shortstop, and the shortstop replaces each ball for the next fielder. Repeat the drill several times.

Comment — Infielders receive excellent base coverage practice. The coach can stop play and make corrections at any time. Have the third baseman act as cut-off man for Ball 1; the first baseman cuts-off Ball 2 and Ball 3.

Let runners lead off from base. Make sure the catcher and runners wear protective equipment. Remind outfielders to think ahead and make overhand throws to the right base.

Time — 20 to 25 minutes.

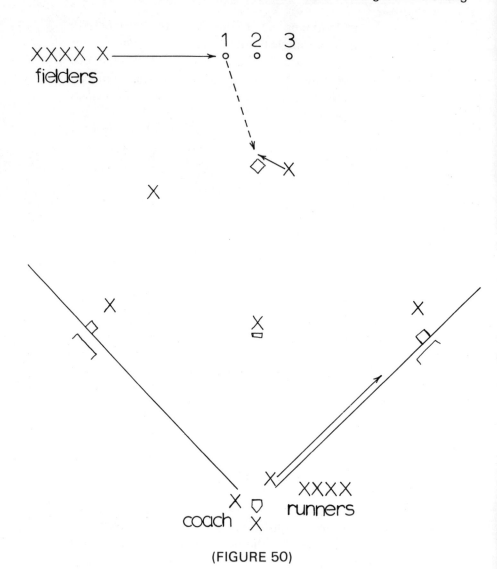

(FIGURE 50)

82. Hit the Towel Game

Objective — To practice making single-bounce throws.

Procedure — Outfielders go to the field. They stand about 200 feet away from a side line fence. The coach or designated player ties a cloth towel (2 feet by 1 foot) on the fence approximately 3 feet above the ground. The towel gives the outfielders a throwing target. Player 1, retriever, collects the balls thrown into the fence. He also judges each thrown ball. Player 2, feeder, tosses balls to the fielder. He stands about 50 feet in front of the fielders. (Figure 51.)

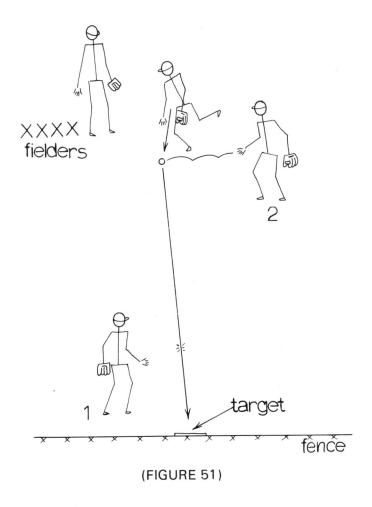

XXXX
fielders

2

1

target

fence

(FIGURE 51)

Action begins when the feeder calls "Go." He tosses a ball in front of the fielder. *Note:* The feeder may throw a fly ball or ground ball. The player fields and makes a single-bounce throw to the target. If the ball strikes the target, the fielder receives 2 points. Each athlete makes 3 throws before rotating in the following manner: Fielder becomes retriever, retriever becomes feeder, and feeder goes to the end of the fielding line. The player who earns the most points wins.

Comment — Remind outfielders to use a cross-seam grip and throw overhand with a complete follow-through.

Time — 15 to 20 minutes.

83. High Fly

Objective — To catch fly balls in a throwing position.

Procedure — Outfielders go to the field. The back-up man, pitcher or manager, stands near the coach. A relay man stays between the fielder and back-up man. Give outfielders these points:

- Test wind direction by throwing pieces of grass into the air. Adjust fielding position accordingly.
- When the ball leaves the bat, run to where you think the ball will land. *Note:* An outfielder learns this through experience.
- Get body under the ball quickly. Be ready to field in a throwing position.
- As the ball comes down, keep body moving forward. Try to line up body in the direction of the throw. This will add power to the throw.

    Have each athlete, in turn, field several fly balls and make overhand, single-bounce throws to the back-up man.

Time — 10 to 15 minutes.

84. Over

Objective — To practice catching balls hit over the fielder's head.

Procedure — Outfielders go to the field. The back-up man, pitcher or manager, stays near the coach. A relay man stands between the fielder and back-up man. Go over the following points with outfielders:

- Test the wind by throwing pieces of grass into the air. Adjust fielding position accordingly.
- When the ball leaves the bat, turn around quickly and run to where you think the ball will land.

Note: Advise fielders not to run backwards. Two things usually happen: (1) the fielder slows down; (2) the player trips and falls.

- A player learns only through experience the approximate area where a long fly ball will land. Wind speed, wind direction, size of the batter, and a batter's stance and swing help a fielder decide where to play in the outfield.
- Never run after a ball with arm and glove extended. This cuts down on running speed. Wait until the last minute before reaching up to make the catch.
- Always try to face the ball while making a play.

Have each player take turns fielding several long hits and making overhand throws to the relay man. The relay man turns and throws to the back-up man. After the play, fielder becomes relay man, and relay man goes to the end of the fielding line.

Time — 10 to 15 minutes.

85. Long Fly Game

Objective — To practice catching balls hit over the fielder's head.

Procedure — Outfielders go to the field. The back-up man, pitcher or manager, stays near the coach. A relay man stands between the fielder and back-up man.

Action begins when the coach fungos a long fly ball over the fielder's head. The fielder turns and runs to where he thinks the ball will land. He stops, turns around, and faces the ball. After catching the ball, the player makes an overhand throw to the relay man. Award points as follows:

0 Points — Misjudges ball, e.g., stops too soon or runs too far. Ball either drops in front of player or lands behind him.

1 Point — A player takes 4 steps or less after turning around to catch the ball.

2 Points — A player takes 2 steps or less after turning around to catch the ball.

4 Points — A player fields the ball in the spot where he turns around to make the catch.

Rule: A player cannot watch the ball while run-ning after it. If he does, he loses all of his points.

Comment — Athletes judge one another. Each player keeps track of his own score. Give each athlete several turns. Players rotate after every play, i.e., fielder becomes relay man and relay man goes to the end of the line. The athlete with the most points wins.

Time — 15 to 20 minutes.

86. Up and Back

Objective — To practice fielding and throwing.

Procedure — Outfielders go to the field. Player 1, tosser, stands about 100 feet ahead of the fielders. (Figure 52.)

Action begins when the tosser hollers "Go." A fielder runs forward at full speed. When he passes Player 1, Player 1 tosses a fly ball to the fielder. The athlete fields and makes an overhand throw to Player 1. After the throw, the fielder sprints back to his original starting place. Player 1 tosses a fly ball to the fielder. The athlete fields and makes an overhand throw to Player 1. After catching 2 balls, the fielder becomes tosser and tosser goes to the end of the line. Each athlete should toss, field, and throw several times.

Time — 15 to 20 minutes.

87. Reaction Game

Objective — To practice fielding and throwing.

Procedure — Outfielders go to the field. The coach and back-up man (manager or pitcher) stand about 150 feet away.

Action begins when a player takes his fielding stance. Have each athlete do 3 things:
- Crouch low keeping body weight forward.
- Keep arms extended out in front of body.
- Remain still until the coach hits the ball.

The coach fungos a ball to the fielder. After the ball leaves the bat, the coach yells "Go," and the

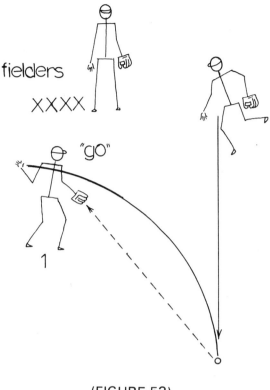

fielders

XXXX

"go"

1

(FIGURE 52)

player fields and throws to the back-up man. Award points as follows:

1 Point — Athlete makes a routine play, i.e., catches a pop fly or fields a ground ball.

2 Points — Athlete makes a shoestring catch or a leaping overhead catch.

The first player earning 15 or more points wins. An athlete loses his points if he moves before the coach hollers "Go," makes a fielding error, or makes a poor throw to the back-up man. After the play, the fielder goes to the line.

Comment — Give each player several turns. Repeat the activity often.

Time — 20 to 25 minutes.

88. Roll and Throw

Objective — To practice making overhand throws to home plate.

Procedure — Outfielders and infielders go to their positions. Outfielders, playing medium deep, bring a ball with them. Runners (extra players) gather near second base. *Note:* Use only 2 or 3 runners at a time. The coach stands behind the pitcher's mound.

Action begins when the coach yells "Go," and the runner takes off for third. The left fielder tosses a ball several feet to his left or to his right, charges the ball, fields, and throws the ball to home plate. The runner tries to score on the play.

Play continues as the center fielder and right fielder follow the same procedure. Let each outfielder make 3 or 4 throws. The cut-off men return balls to the outfielders.

Comment — Have the third baseman cut-off throws from left field and the first baseman cut-off throws from center and right. Be sure catcher and runners wear protective equipment. Allow slow runners to get a good jump from second base.

Time — 15 to 20 minutes.

6

Improving Hitting and Bunting with Drills and Games

The Batter

Possibly the single toughest skill in baseball to teach is hitting. A batter, like a computer, is most effective when all of his circuits are working. The stance, stride, and swing make up a large part of this circuitry.

An alert coach watches his hitters carefully. He realizes that finding and correcting batting flaws can be extremely difficult. One problem a coach faces is overcoaching, i.e., confusing the athlete by having him work on too many things at once. Perhaps the best remedy is to have the athlete concentrate on one thing at a time until he gains confidence in his hitting ability.

The following activities include drills and games that help an athlete improve his bunting and hitting skills. A special section, *Hitting Problems and Ways to Solve Them,* describes some common batting faults and how to correct them.

89. On Deck Exercises

Objective — To prepare muscles for swinging the bat.
Procedure — Bring a leaded bat, bat and donut, or regular bat to the on-deck circle. Try these 4 exercises:

Exercise Number 1
- Place both hands around the bat handle. Stand with feet apart.
- Press fat end of bat into the ground. Lean forward keeping arms straight and wrists stiff.
- Bring body weight over hands while pressing down on the bat. (Figure 53.) Hold position for 5 seconds. Return to standing position. (Figure 53.)
- Repeat 5 or 6 times.

Time — 30 seconds.

(FIGURE 53)

Exercise Number 2
- Hold the bat at both ends. Rest the middle of the bat against the back of neck. Stand with feet together.
- Lean forward, bend at the knees, and touch chin to knees. (Figure 54.)
- Return to standing position.
- Repeat 5 or 6 times.

Time — 30 seconds

(FIGURE 54)

Exercise Number 3

- Stand with feet spread apart shoulder-width.
- Grip the bat with both hands. Extend arms toward the ground. Begin swinging the bat back and forth. (Figure 55A and B.)
- Continue moving the bat back and forth. Keep arms fully extended.
- Make 3 complete circles to the left bringing the end of the bat over the head. Go 3 times to the right.
- Repeat 2 or 3 times.

Time — 30 seconds.

(FIGURE 55A)

(FIGURE 55B)

Exercise Number 4
- Stand with feet spread apart shoulder-width.
- Grip the bat handle with one hand. Make 3 complete overhead swings keeping the arm fully extended. (Figure 56.) Grab the bat with both hands and take 3 hard swings at an imaginary pitch. Now hold the bat with the opposite hand and make 3 full overhead swings.
- Repeat 2 or 3 times.

Time — 30 seconds.

90. Tee Target

Objective — To practice hitting off the tee.

Procedure — Place a batting tee about 15 feet in front of a side line fence. Tie 2 pieces of cloth (1 square foot) half way up the fence — one to the left and one to the right of the batting tee. Alternate adjusting the tee for low inside and high inside pitches. Hit 5 balls at the left side target.

Alternate adjusting the tee for low outside and high outside pitches and hit 5 balls at the right side target. Record each time the ball hits the target. Repeat several times.

(FIGURE 56)

Comment — Urge athletes to hold their heads still, watch the ball, and swing the bat with a complete follow-through.
Time — 10 to 15 minutes.

91. Quick Stick

Objective — To practice hitting off the tee.
Procedure — Place the batting tee about 15 feet in front of a side line fence. Find a partner. Have him hold 5 baseballs.

Play Quick Stick, a competitive batting tee game. Partner 1, batter, takes his batting stance. Partner 2, feeder, sets the baseballs, one at a time, on the tee. The hitter drives each ball into the fence. The feeder places the balls on the tee in rapid succession. *Note:* Tell the feeder to back out of the way before the hitter swings the bat. Award points as follows:

1 Point — A clean hit, either line drive or ground ball, into the fence.

0 Points — A swing and miss, foul ball, or a swing that breaks the tee.

Go 5 rounds. The athlete earning the most points wins.

Comment — Have players use a choke grip on the bat. This will help them bring the bat around faster. Remind them to keep their eyes on the ball.

Time — 10 to 15 minutes.

92. Partner Lob

Objective — To practice hitting the ball.

Procedure — Two athletes, Player 1 and Player 2, take turns hitting the ball into a fence. Player 1, hitter, stands about 20 feet from the side line fence. Player 2, tosser, stays to one side and lobs the ball to Player 1 (Figure 57). The batter hits the ball into the fence. Each player hits several balls apiece.

Comment — Have the tosser stand to the right of right-hand hitters and to the left of left-hand hitters.

Time — 10 to 15 minutes.

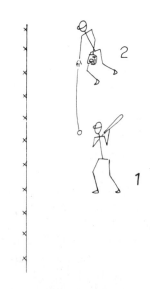

fence

(FIGURE 57)

93. Double Lob

Objective — To practice bunting and hitting the ball.

Procedure — Three athletes, Players 1, 2, and 3, take turns hitting and bunting the ball into a fence. Player 1, hitter, stands about 20 feet from the side line fence. Players 2 and 3, tossers, stay to each side of Player 1 (Figure 58). The batter bunts the first toss and hits the second toss into the fence. After 8 swings (including bunts), athletes rotate clockwise. Player 1 becomes Player 2, Player 2 becomes Player 3, and Player 3 becomes Player 1.

Comment — As a safety precaution, have the tosser who delivers the bunt pitch stand to the hitting side of the batter.

Time — 10 to 15 minutes.

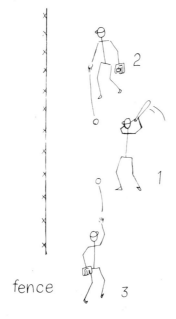

(FIGURE 58)

94. Five Minute Hit

Objective — To combine hitting and fielding.

Procedure — Divide the team into 2 groups, A and B, 9 players (optional) per group. Keep each team balanced, e.g., pitcher, catcher, 4 infielders, and 3 outfielders. Group A, offense, comes to bat with each athlete spending 5 minutes at a different station. The chart shows the station, time, location, and player responsibility. Figure 59 shows the position of the stations.

Station	Time (min.)	Location	Player Responsibility
1	5	Home plate	Hits live pitches
2	5	Behind batting cage	On deck batting exercise (Drill 89)
3	5	Right side line fence	Hits off batting tee (Drill 90 — with or without target)
4	5	Right side line fence	Tosser for Partner Lob (Drill 92)
5	5	Right side line fence	Hitter for Partner Lob (Drill 92)
6	5	Left field foul line	Back-up man for hitter
7	5	Left field foul line	Fungo balls to outfielders
8	5	Left side of batting cage	Back-up man for hitter
9	5	Left side of batting cage	Fungo balls to infielders

Five Minute Hit

Group B athletes, the defense, play their regular positions. They work on fielding techniques. Infielders practice fielding, throwing, setting up relays and cutting-off throws from the outfield. Outfielders practice catching fly balls, fielding ground

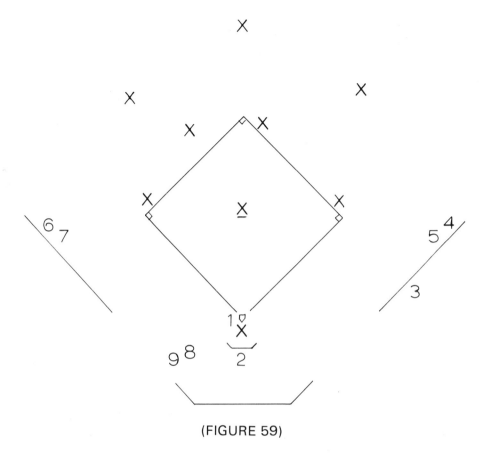

(FIGURE 59)

balls, backing up each other, and making overhand throws.

The pitcher throws one-half to three-quarters speed. He alternates pitching from a stretch and wind-up position. The catcher, wearing full protective gear, moves his target around the strike zone. *Suggestion:* Let pitcher throw to only 4 or 5 batters. Have another hurler or player throw to the remaining hitters.

Pitching strategy varies. Here's a simple plan: Have the pitcher throw straight balls for 2 minutes, a mixture of straight and breaking pitches for 2 minutes, and breaking pitches only for the last minute.

The coach keeps time. After 5 minutes, athletes

rotate, i.e., Station 9 to Station 1, Station 1 to Station 2, Station 2 to Station 3, and so on. After Team A hits, change sides. Group A takes the field; Group B comes to bat and goes through the stations.

Comment — The drill may accommodate a larger number of players, but it works best with 14 to 18 athletes. Every player has something to do and the coach stays busy helping athletes with hitting and fielding problems. Remind fungo batters to stay alert and hit balls between pitches, not when the hitter is swinging at a ball. Make certain batters wear protective helmets. Keep players hustling. Too much delay lengthens the drill.

Time — One hour and forty-five minutes.

95. Five Minute Hit/Five Minute Bunt

Objective — To combine hitting, bunting, and fielding.

Procedure — Repeat Drill 94. Make the following change: Substitute Station 2, On-Deck Batting Exercises, with live pitch bunting. Move Station 2 from behind the batting cage to the right side line fence near first base. A player, acting as pitcher, stands about 30 feet away and faces the batter. The batter concentrates on bunting the ball to the left, to the right, and back to the pitcher.

Time — One hour and forty-five minutes.

96. Double Hit and Bunt

Objective — To combine hitting, bunting, and fielding.

Procedure — Divide the team into 2 groups, A and B, 9 players (optional) per group. Group B, defense, positions themselves according to Figure 60. *Note:* Three pitchers work this drill. Two throw hitting practice; one tosses live bunting practice. Have pitchers throw without catchers. Let catchers play in the field. Group A, offense, comes to bat. Each athlete spends 5 minutes at a different station. The chart shows the station, time, location, and player responsibility:

Station	Time (min.)	Location	Player Responsibility
1	5	Left side of batting cage	Hit live pitches
2	5	Right field side line fence	Bunt live pitches
3	5	Right side of batting cage	Hit live pitches
4	5	Left field side line fence	Hits off batting tee (Drill 90 — with or without target)
5	5	Between Station 4 and Station 1	Hitter for Partner Lob (Drill 92 — *Note:* Use manager for tosser)
6	5	Left field foul line	Back-up man for hitter
7	5	Left field foul line	Fungo balls to outfielders
8	5	Right field foul line	Back-up man for hitter
9	5	Right field foul line	Fungo balls to infielders

Double Hit and Bunt

Group B infielders practice fielding and throwing. The third baseman returns balls to the left side pitcher; the first baseman returns balls to the right side pitcher. Outfielders practice catching fly balls, fielding ground balls, backing up each other, and making overhand throws.

The pitcher throws one-half to three-quarters speed. He alternates pitching from a stretch and wind-up position. *Suggestion:* Let pitchers throw to only 4 or 5 batters. Have them share pitching chores with the catchers. Tell pitchers to mix throwing straight balls with breaking pitches (See suggested plan, Drill 94).

The coach keeps time. After 5 minutes, athletes rotate, i.e., Station 9 to Station 1, Station 1 to Station 2, Station 2 to Station 3, and so on. After team A hits, sides change. Group A takes the field; Group B comes to bat.

Comment — See Comment, Drill 94. Remind fungo batters that 2 hitters are swinging. Tell them not to fungo balls when batters are swinging. *Suggestion:* Place a net or screen between the batting cage and backstop. The net protects hitters from balls bouncing off the backstop from opposite directions. Old fishing nets or blankets supported on boards make a satisfactory shield.

Time — One hour and forty-five minutes.

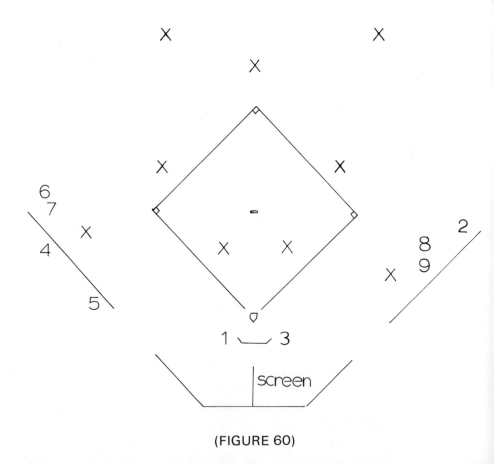

(FIGURE 60)

97. Three Inning Hitting Game

Objective — To combine hitting, bunting, and fielding.

Procedure — Divide the team into Groups A and B, 9 players (optional) per group. Group A, offense, comes to home plate. Group B, defense, takes the field. Game rules are as follows:

- Each player on the offensive team comes to bat 3 times per inning. He receives 3 swings or 3 chances to hit the ball.

- He runs out every hit. He may reach base safely on hits, errors, walks, catcher's interference, or when struck by a pitched ball.

- A runner may advance on errors, hits, walks, sacrifice flies, bunts, passed balls, wild pitches, catcher's interference, or when the pitcher hits the batter. *Note:* Do not let runners steal or pitchers give intentional walks. Allow runners to lead off from base.

- If a runner or batter makes an out, he returns to the end of the line and bats in turn.

- A batter walks when the pitcher fails to throw a strike on 2 consecutive pitches.

- A hitter strikes out when he takes a called strike or fouls a pitch.

- Runners clear the bases after 3 outs. Sides change when the last hitter completes his third time at bat. Athletes rotate. Group B comes to bat; Group A takes the field.

- The pitcher throws one-half to three-quarters speed.

- The game lasts 3 innings. Each team keeps track of its own score. The team with the most runs wins. Regardless of score, both teams complete their time at bat.

Comment — Have extra players work in small groups or umpire until they enter the game. Make sure hitters and runners wear protective helmets. Remind catchers to wear full protective gear. Urge offensive and defensive players to try various game strategies. Keep athletes hustling on and off the field.

Time — One hour and forty-five minutes.

98. Four Group Shift Game

Objective — To combine hitting, bunting, and fielding.

Procedure — Divide athletes into 4 teams, 5 players (optional) per team. Assign a pitcher for each team. Team 1 comes to bat; Teams 2, 3 and 4 position themselves according to Figure 61. *Note:* Team 4 stays behind the right field side line fence and practices bunting.

Athletes take turns pitching, fielding, and bunting. Each player spends approximately three and one-half minutes bunting balls down the right field side line. A Team 4 player stands near the left field line and fungos to the outfielders between pitches. (Use team manager for back-up man.)

Game rules are as follows:

- Team 1 players take turns hitting for 15 minutes. Each batter receives 1 swing or 1 chance to hit a strike-zone ball per time at bat. Teams 2 and 3 play defense.
- The batter runs out every hit. He may reach base safely on a hit or error. A hitter cannot take his base if he is struck by the ball.
- Do not allow walks. A batter remains at the plate until he hits the ball into fair territory, fouls off the pitch, or swings and misses.
- The pitcher throws one-half to three-quarters speed.
- A runner may advance on errors, hits, sacrifice flies, and bunts. Do not allow runners to lead off or steal.
- If a runner or batter makes an out, he returns to the end of the line and takes his turn at bat.
- A hitter strikes out when he fouls off the pitch or swings and misses.
- Runners clear the bases after 3 outs. After 15 minutes, teams change in the following manner: Team 1 becomes Team 4, Team 4 becomes Team 3, Team 3 becomes Team 2, and Team 2 becomes Team 1.
- Each team hits 2 rounds, 15 minutes per round.

Comment — Keep players hustling at all times. Have pitchers concentrate on throwing strikes. *Note:* Pitchers throw into the batting cage. Let catchers play in the outfield.

It's tough to score many runs with 10 men on defense. Urge hitters to use offensive strategy, i.e., sacrifice bunt, squeeze bunt, hit and run, etc. Have pitchers cover home on all plays at home plate.

Time — Two hours.

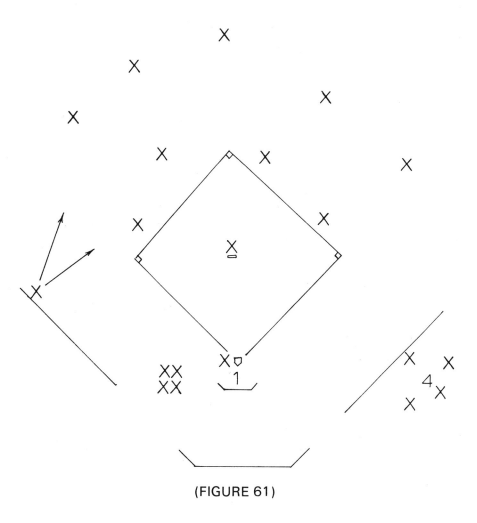

(FIGURE 61)

99. Thirty — Forty — Fifty

Objective — To combine hitting, bunting, and fielding.

Procedure — Divide athletes into 4 teams, 5 players (optional) per team. Spread teams around the field, preferably near a fence or backstop area. Have players bring a rubber base (home plate), gloves, and 2 or 3 balls with them.

Action begins when Player 1 comes to home plate. Player 2, pitcher, stands about 30 feet away from the hitter. He throws straight pitches one-half to three-quarters speed. *Note:* Do not allow pitchers to lob the ball; lobbing throws off the batter's timing. Player 1 bunts 2 balls to Player 3 and bunts 2 balls to Player 5. Players 3 and 5 field and throw to Player 4. (Figure 62.) Player 4 returns the balls to Player 2. Athletes rotate clockwise. Player 1 becomes Player 3, Player 3 becomes Player 4, Player 4 becomes Player 5, Player 5 becomes pitcher, and pitcher becomes hitter.

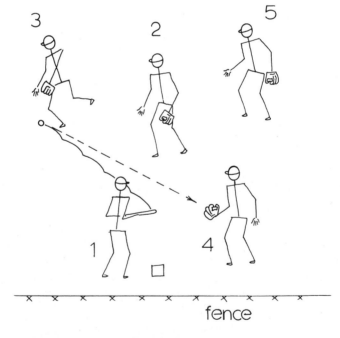

(FIGURE 62)

After each athlete bunts 4 pitches, play continues with the pitcher moving about 40 feet away from the hitter. Players 3, 4 and 5 position themselves accordingly. Player 1, using a choke grip, punches 2 balls to Player 3, 2 balls to Player 4, and 2 balls to Player 5. Fielders return balls to the pitcher. Athletes rotate clockwise.

After each athlete hits 6 pitches, action continues with the pitcher moving about 50 feet away from the hitter. Players 3, 4 and 5 position themselves accordingly. Player 1, using a choke grip, punches 6 balls wherever he chooses. Fielders return balls to the pitcher. Athletes rotate clockwise.

Comment — If chasing foul balls become a problem, position a fielder behind the fence to retrieve the balls. He can be on-deck batter and swing a bat while waiting his turn to hit.

This activity requires the athlete to keep his eye on the ball, hold his head still, and use a choke grip. A choke grip helps cut down on the swing and enables the batter to make solid contact with the ball.

Keep groups spread far enough apart to prevent players from running into each other.

Time — Forty-five minutes to one hour.

100. Swack

Objective — To combine hitting, bunting, and fielding.

Procedure — Divide the team into Groups A and B, 9 players (optional) per group. Group A, offense, comes to home plate. Group B, defense, takes the field. Group A athletes alternate hitting and bunting. For example, Player 1 swings away, Player 2 bunts, Player 3 swings away, Player 4 bunts, and so on. Each athlete receives 4 chances per round to hit and bunt. After 1 round, teams change sides. Group A takes the field; Group B comes to bat.

Give athletes these guidelines:

• The batter stays at the plate until he hits or bunts

the ball into fair territory. He must run out each hit or bunt.

- Regular baseball rules apply. *Exceptions:* Batters do not walk. They cannot take first on catcher's interference or when struck by a pitched ball. Allow runners to lead off from base and steal.
- The pitcher throws one-half to three-quarters speed.
- If a runner or batter makes an out, he returns to the end of the line and bats in turn.
- Runners clear the bases after 3 outs. Regardless of number of outs, teams change sides after 1 round. Each team bats for 3 rounds.
- Teams keep track of their scores. Let the losing team run laps, do push-ups, or put away equipment.

Comment — Urge offensive and defensive players to try various game strategies. Have extra players work in small groups or umpire until they enter the game. Make sure hitters, runners, and catchers wear protective equipment. *Suggestion:* Keep offensive athletes busy. Have them swing a weighted bat or hit off the tee until they come to the plate.

Time — One hour and forty-five minutes.

101. Bat Control Game

Objective — To practice bat control.

Procedure — Divide players into groups of 3. Send groups next to the backstop or fences. Each group brings balls, gloves, and bats with them. Players 2 and 3, fielders, stay about 40 feet apart. Player 1, hitter, stands approximately 50 to 60 feet away from the fielders. (Figure 63.)

Action starts when either Player 2 or Player 3 throws the ball to Player 1. Player 1, using a choke grip, receives 12 swings or 12 chances to hit the ball according to the charted plan.

Follow these game rules:

- The hitter swings at strikes only. If he fouls or

Swing	Where batter hits ball	How batter hits ball
1	Player 2	Soft liner
2	Player 3	Soft liner
3	Player 2	Soft liner
4	Player 3	Soft liner
5	Player 2	Single hopper
6	Player 3	Single hopper
7	Player 2	Single hopper
8	Player 3	Single hopper
9	Player 2	Two hopper
10	Player 3	Two hopper
11	Player 2	Two hopper
12	Player 3	Two hopper

Bat Control Game

misses the pitch, it counts as a swing. He must continue to hit according to plan.
- The batter receives one point for each successful hit.
- Batter must use a choke grip. If he fails to do so, he loses all of his points.
- The game lasts 3 rounds (optional). Each athlete comes to bat once each round.
- Athletes keep track of their scores. The player with the most points wins.

Comment — Remind athletes that a choke grip cuts down on bat
speed and gives the hitter more control over the bat.
　　Time — 30 to 40 minutes.

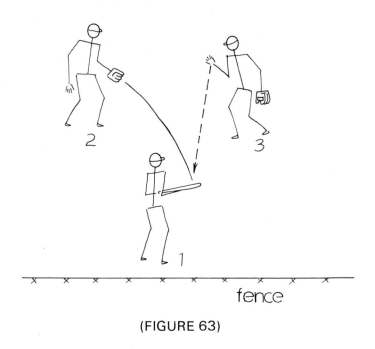

(FIGURE 63)

Hitting Problems and Ways to Solve Them

Batting problems occur throughout the season. The following
nine drills offer suggestions for helping individual players overcome
their hitting difficulties. Include these points with each drill:

- Send a pitcher, catcher, and fielder to the diamond. Have
  the player swing a bat while the pitcher warms up.
- Tell the athlete to take a comfortable stance, choke up on
  the bat, and use a firm, but relaxed grip.
- Add the competitive factor. Set up a point game. Give the
  hitter one point for every ball he hits into fair territory.
  Give the pitcher two points when the hitter takes a strike,
  fouls a pitch, swings at bad pitches, or swings and misses.
  Let the catcher keep score.
- Have the catcher closely observe the hitter. Tell him to stop
  play and make corrections when necessary.

102. Too Many Pitches

Objective — To keep the batter from taking too many pitches.
Procedure — When the pitcher is ready, the athlete comes to home
plate. Give him these guidelines:
- Before the pitcher throws the first ball, extend the
bat across home plate. Tap the outside corner of
plate with the fat end of the bat. Adjust stance to
make sure bat covers home plate.
- Study the strike zone. Form a mental picture of the
area between the shoulders and knees. Decide to
swing at pitches that enter this zone.
- Watch the ball hit the catcher's mitt. Do this for
6 to 8 pitches. Do not swing at the ball. *Note:* Tell
pitcher to move the ball around the strike zone.
- Mentally judge each pitch. For example, say to
yourself: "Strike." "Ball on low, outside corner."
Check each pitch with the catcher.
- Repeat procedure. Swing easy. Try to hit pitches
up the middle of the diamond. Swing hard enough
to meet the ball in front of home plate.
Comment — The competitive factor helps the batter concentrate
on the pitched ball. If possible, work with hitters before or after practice. Urge athletes to work on their
own. It's important that athletes understand the value
of extra practice.

103. High Pitches

Objective — To keep the batter from swinging at high pitches.
Procedure — When the pitcher is ready, the athlete comes to home
plate. Give him these guidelines:
- Lengthen stance by moving the lead foot closer to
the pitcher.
- Crouch by bending at the knees. Keep body weight
distributed over both feet. *Note:* Crouching nar-
rows the strike zone and helps the batter see the
ball better.
- Watch the ball hit the catcher's mitt. Do this for 6
to 8 pitches. Do not swing at the ball. Check each

pitch with the catcher. *Note:* Have the pitcher throw high strikes.

- Repeat procedure. Swing easy. Try to hit pitches up the middle of the diamond. Swing hard enough to meet the ball in front of home plate.

Comment — Show the batter the difference between a high strike and a high pitch out of the strike zone. Very often a high pitch fools the hitter. At the last second it rises or sails out of the strike zone. If the batter doesn't watch the ball carefully, he'll probably swing at the pitch. (See Comment, Drill 102.)

Time — Varies with individual.

104. Short Swing

Objective — To help the player swing with a complete follow-through.

Procedure — When the pitcher is ready, the athlete comes to home plate. Give him these guidelines:

- Try to relax. Many hitters become too tense and swing the bat in a stiff, choppy manner.
- Take 2 or 3 deep breaths. *Note:* Not all coaches agree that deep breathing helps the batter. Ask the player how he feels. If he thinks deep breathing is beneficial, let him continue.
- Form a mental picture of the strike zone. Make up mind to swing at pitches in the strike zone. Hit 8 to 10 balls up the middle of the diamond.
- Concentrate on taking a smooth, full swing at the ball. Try to see the ball hit the bat.

Comment — An aggressive hitter goes after the ball. He decides beforehand to hit the ball where it's pitched. A confused batter shows his indecision by taking good pitches, swinging weakly at the ball, or swinging at any ball the pitcher throws. See Comment, Drill 102.

Time — Varies with individual

105. Pop Up

Objective — To keep the batter from popping up too often.

Procedure — When the pitcher is ready, the athlete comes to home plate. Give him these guidelines:
- Swing at 8 to 10 pitches. *Note:* Tell the pitcher to throw high strikes at three-quarters speed. The batter will probably pop up or swing and miss.
- Adjust the hitter's stance. Have him slightly raise the shoulder that points away from the pitcher. Elevating the shoulder lifts the bat, lowers the head, and gives the batter a good look at the pitch.
- Swing down on the ball. Hit several pitches up the middle of the diamond.

Comment — Show the hitter that swinging down on the ball is actually a level swing. This idea is difficult to get across. See Comment, Drill 102.

Time — Varies with individual.

106. Weak Ground Ball

Objective — To help the batter make solid contact with the pitched ball.

Procedure — When the pitcher is ready, the athlete comes to home plate. Give him these guidelines:
- Take a comfortable stance. Line up the middle knuckles of both hands. This grip allows smooth wrist rotation and adds power to the swing. *Note:* A smart hurler will jam the hitter who uses a tight grip. He knows that a batter using a locked wrist swing will hit inside pitches weakly onto the ground.
- Swing at 8 to 10 pitches. Fully extend arms and hit the ball out in front of home plate. The bat should meet the ball at the moment the weight changes from the back foot to the front foot. *Suggestion:* Tell pitcher to keep balls on the inside corner of home plate.

Comment — See Comment, Drill 102.

Time — Varies with individual.

107. Pulling Head

Objective — To help batter keep his eye on the ball.

Procedure — When the pitcher is ready, the athlete steps up to the plate. Give him these guidelines:
- Watch the ball from the time it leaves the pitcher's hand until it hits the catcher's mitt. Stride with the lead foot pointing toward the pitcher. Do not swing at the pitch. Repeat 3 or 4 times.
- Repeat procedure. Hit 8 to 10 pitches. Drive the ball up the middle of the diamond. *Suggestion:* Paint the fat end of several bats a bright color. Tell the player to watch the ball hit the colored part of the bat.

Comment — See Comment, Drill 102.

Time — Varies with individual.

108. Too Many Strike Outs

Objective — To help the batter cut down on number of strike outs.

Procedure — When the pitcher is ready, the athlete comes to home plate. Give him these guidelines:
- Study the strike zone. Form a mental picture of the area between the shoulders and knees. Make up mind to swing at strikes.
- Follow the ball into the catcher's mitt. Repeat for several pitches. Do not swing at the ball.
- Repeat procedure. Swing at 8 to 10 pitches. Wait until the last second to hit the ball. Bring the bat around quickly. *Note:* Remind batter to use a choke grip for bat control.

Comment — The hitter must keep his eye on the ball. If he doesn't, a late swing won't help him improve. It may take the hitter 3 or 4 rounds to adjust.

Time — Varies with individual.

109. Pulling Outside Pitch

Objective — To keep the batter from pulling outside pitches.

Procedure — When the pitcher is ready, the athlete comes to home plate. Give him these guidelines:
- Follow the ball into the catcher's mitt. Repeat for 6 to 8 pitches. Do not swing at the ball.

- Repeat procedure. *Note:* Tell pitcher to throw balls on the outside corner.
- Swing easy. Fully extend arms. Hit the ball out in front of home plate. Go with the pitch. For example, hit outside pitch into right field (right-handed hitter) or hit outside pitch into left field (left-handed hitter).

Comment — See Comment, Drill 102.

Time — Varies with individual.

110. Loss of Timing

Objective — To help a batter properly time the pitch.

Procedure — When the pitcher is ready, the athlete comes up to the plate. Give him these guidelines:

- Take a comfortable stance. Line up the middle knuckles of each hand. Relax.
- Bunt 8 to 10 pitches out in front of home plate. Watch the ball hit the bat.
- Use a choke grip, swing easy, and hit several balls up the middle of home plate. Hit the ball when the weight shifts from the back foot to the front foot. Follow-through completely with each swing.
- Repeat procedure. Bring the bat around faster. Be careful not to overstride or pull the lead foot to the side. Pulling the lead foot forces the head away from the ball.
- Continue swinging until the bat makes solid contact with the ball.

Comment — Remind athlete that patience and hard work pay off.

Time — Varies with individual.

Here is a list of items that will help the coach plan his hitting practices:

- Organize practice in advance. Each player should know where he is supposed to be and what he is expected to do. Spend 10 to 15 minutes going over the practice schedule.
- Keep all players busy during batting practice. This can be an enormous task. Have athletes take turns hitting fungos to the outfielders and infielders. Let players waiting to bat hit off the tee, swing a weighted bat, practice On-Deck Exer-

cises (Drill 89), or play Partner Lob (Drill 92) or Double Lob (Drill 93).

- Use a variety of activities. Check the drills offered in Chapter 7: *Keeping Players Sharp with Competitive Team Games.*
- Keep athletes hustling on and off the field. Be sure players understand their roles in competitive games and drills.
- Stay on schedule. Start and stop activities on time.

The Bunter

Players often neglect spending enough time on bunting practice. Some athletes feel bunting is less important than hitting because they are seldom called upon to bunt.

The coach's attitude plays a big part in getting players to work on their bunting. If he believes bunting is important, he must convince his athletes by offering bunting drills in practice. A simple philosophy is: Score one run at a time; use the bunt to get men into scoring position.

The following games will help the player improve his bunting skills:

111. Drop It Game

Objective — To practice bunting the ball.
Procedure — Divide players into groups of 4. Send groups near the backstop or fence. Each group brings balls, gloves, and bats with them. Player 2, pitcher, stands about 40 feet away from Player 1, hitter. Player 3, fielder, stays to the right of Player 2. Player 4, fielder, stays to the left of Player 2. Rags or towels make suitable base lines.

Action begins when the pitcher, throwing at half speed, delivers a ball to the hitter. The batter bunts the ball down either base line. He receives one point if the ball stays in fair territory. If he pops up, fouls, or misses the pitch, he receives no points. The hitter keeps track of his points. After 6 chances, athletes rotate. Player 1 becomes Player 2, Player 2 becomes Player 3, Player 3 becomes Player 4, and Player 4 becomes Player 1. Each athlete comes to bat 2 times. The pitcher throws three-quarters speed during the second round. The athlete earning the most points wins.

Comment — Circulate among the groups. Offer help to those players having trouble. Keep a look out for these problems:

- Failure to hold bat level. The player who tilts or drops the end of his bat is likely to foul off the pitch. (Figure 64.)

(FIGURE 64)

- Bat held too close to body. (Figure 65A.) The batter doesn't get a good look at the ball. He will likely foul off many pitches. The hitter should hold the bat well out in front of home plate. (Figure 65B.)
- Hitter pulls the bat back. The batter should hold his arms straight until he bunts the ball. *Note:* A successful bunter crouches slightly and flexes his arms at the elbow.
- Hitter turns and faces the pitcher too soon. A smart pitcher, with men on base, will attempt a fake pick-off to see if the batter intends to bunt. A batter gives himself away by dropping the bat head or

(FIGURE 65A.)   (FIGURE 65B.)

sliding his hands up the bat handle. The hitter should shift to a bunting position just before the pitcher releases the ball. *Exception:* The hitter waits until the ball leaves the pitcher's hand before squaring around on a suicide squeeze play.

- Batter bunts the ball too hard. The hitter is probably gripping the bat too tight with his upper hand. The bat should rest lightly between thumb and fingers.
- Hitter bunts too many balls foul. Check his body position in the batter's box. He may be standing back too far. Move him into the front part of the batter's box. *Note:* Have players try the pivot position and square around position. Let them select which foot position works best for them.

Time — 30 minutes.

112. Sacrifice Score Game

Objective — To practice bunting the ball.

Procedure — Divide players into groups of 4. Send groups near the backstop or fence. Each group brings balls, gloves, bats, and old towels or rags for bases. (If available, use rubber bases.) Each group sets up a diamond with bases approximately 60 feet apart and pitcher's mound about 40 feet away from home plate. Fielders position themselves according to Figure 66.

Action begins when 2 groups meet. Group 1, offense, comes to home plate. Group 2, defense, takes the field. Game rules are as follows:

- The pitcher throws at three-quarters speed. Do not allow hurler to lob the ball. Slow pitching throws off a batter's timing.
- The offensive team bunts for 10 minutes. Batters must hit in turn. For example, if bases are loaded and the fourth hitter strikes out, the first batter must leave third base, come to home plate, and hit.
- The batter stays at home plate until he bunts the ball or makes an out. He runs out balls bunted into fair territory.
- A player makes an out when he pops up, fouls, or misses the pitch.
- Runners may slide. They cannot lead off or steal.
- Player 1, pitcher, is the only player allowed to field bunts. Players 2, 3 and 4 must stay near their bases. Their job is to tag out runners.
- Let defensive players change positions whenever they wish. Switching positions keeps the drill interesting.
- The pitcher makes put-outs at home plate. He must tag out the runner.
- Runners clear the bases after 3 outs. Teams keep track of their own score. The team with the most runs after 2 rounds wins.
- Sides change after 10 minutes. Group 1 takes the field; Group 2 comes to bat.

Comment — Remind athletes that runners cannot leave base until the batter bunts the ball. If a runner leaves too soon, he's out, and must return to the end of the line. Make sure batters and runners wear protective equipment.

Time — 45 to 50 minutes.

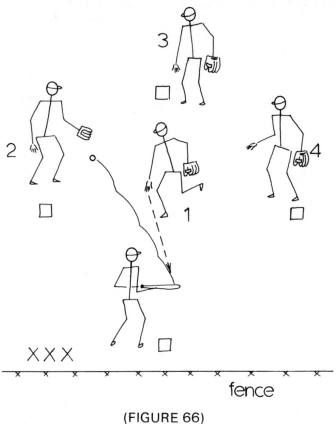

XXX

fence

(FIGURE 66)

113. Partner Bunt Game

Objective — To practice bunting the ball.
Procedure — Divide players into groups of 3. Send groups near the backstop or fence. Each group brings balls, gloves, bats, and a rubber base for first base.

Action begins when 2 groups meet. Group 1, offense, comes to home plate. Group 2, defense, positions itself according to Figure 67. Player 1, pitcher, stands about 40 feet away from the hitter. Player 2, fielder, stays to the right of the pitcher. Player 3, fielder, stays to the left of the pitcher. First base is approximately 70 feet from home plate.

Game rules are as follows:

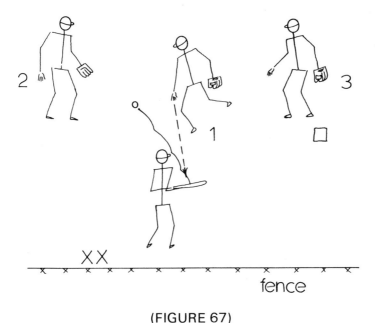

(FIGURE 67)

- The pitcher throws three-quarters speed. He concentrates on throwing strikes.
- The offensive team bunts for 10 minutes. Hitters bunt in order and must run out every ball bunted into fair territory.
- When a player reaches first safely, he must stay there until a teammate bunts him home. If his teammate fails, his teammate is out, and goes to the end of the line and bats in turn.
- Defensive players cannot move until the batter bunts the ball.
- A player makes an out when he pops up, fouls, or misses the pitch.
- Do not allow runners to lead off.
- Player 3 acts as first baseman. Player 2 or the pitcher covers home plate. The runner must be tagged out at home.
- After 3 outs, the runner leaves first base.
- Each team keeps its own score. The team scoring the most runs wins.

- Sides change after 10 minutes. Group 1 takes the field; Group 2 comes to bat. Go 2 rounds.

Comment — Make sure batters and runners wear protective equipment.

Time — 45 to 50 minutes.

114. Rainbow Game

Objective — To practice bunting the ball.

Procedure — Divide players into groups of 4. Send groups near the backstop or fence. Each group brings balls, gloves, bats, rags, towels, rubber base, and lime marking (ground calcium carbonate — $CaCO_3$). Rags or towels mark the base lines, the rubber base represents home plate, and the 3 rainbow-shaped lines — set 5 feet apart — represent target lines. Use lime to make the target lines. (Figure 68.)

Athletes position themselves according to Figure 68. Player 1, hitter, comes to home plate. Player 2, pitcher, stands about 40 feet away from the batter. Player 3, fielder, stays to the right of the pitcher. Player 4, fielder, stays to the left of the pitcher.

Here are the game rules:

- The pitcher throws three-quarters speed.
- The batter receives 6 chances to bunt the ball. He stays at bat until he bunts 6 balls into fair territory.
- Fielders, including pitcher, are not allowed to pick up a bunted ball until it stops rolling. *Exception:* A foul ball.
- Look at the scoring chart. It shows how a batter earns points for bunted balls.
- After 6 bunts, athletes rotate clockwise. Player 1 becomes pitcher, pitcher becomes Player 3, Player 3 becomes Player 4, and Player 4 comes to home plate.
- Athletes keep their own scores. The player with the most points wins.

Comment — Remind hitters to wear protective helmets. Let athletes play 2 or 3 rounds.

Time — 30 to 40 minutes.

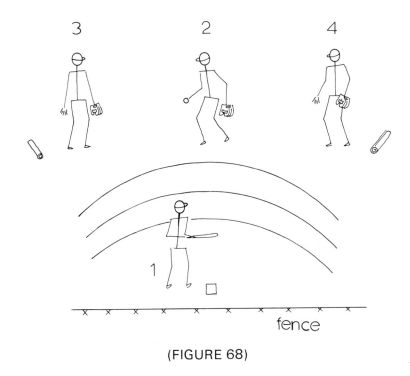

(FIGURE 68)

Points earned	Where the ball comes to rest
6	Between home plate and the first line
5	On the first line
4	Between the first line and the second line
3	On the second line
2	Between the second line and the third line
1	On the third line
0	Beyond the third line

Scoring Chart

7

Keeping Players Sharp with Competitive Team Games

Athletes respond well to challenging activities. This chapter includes 10 competitive games that cover hitting, bunting, fielding, and base running skills.

The following 12 suggestions will help the games run smoothly:

- Divide athletes into 2 teams, 9 players per team.
- Give the offensive team 2 choices: Let players decide in which order they wish to hit or have them bat according to player number, e.g., pitcher first, catcher second, first baseman third, and so forth.
- Tell pitchers to throw at three-quarters speed. Have them mix their pitches. In most of these drills, the pitcher's control is the key to success. A wild thrower slows down action and players soon lose interest. Make sure hurlers warm their arms properly.
- Have pitchers throw from the stretch with men on base.
- Limit hurlers to 4 or 5 warm-up pitches. Too much throwing between rounds prolongs the game.
- Have catchers wear full protective gear, e.g., cup, shin guards, chest protector, and mask. *Exception:* When the catcher plays roving fielder.
- Let the team manager or catcher handle umpiring chores.

- Each team keeps its score. The team with the most points wins. Have the losing squad run laps or do push-ups.
- Let athletes experiment. Urge them to try different offensive and defensive strategy.
- Caution players to wear protective helmets, sliding pads, and long-legged pants.
- Let extra players coach bases, warm-up, or play pepper until they enter the game.
- Keep athletes busy. Have players waiting to hit swing a bat.

115. Three Swing Score

Objective — To practice hitting, bunting, base running, and fielding.
Procedure — The procedure is as follows:
- The defensive team takes the field. The offensive team lines up near home plate.
- Each batter receives 3 swings per round. A round consists of 9 players coming to bat. The hitter is free to bunt or hit any pitch.
- If the batter hits a ball on the third swing into fair territory, he runs it out. *Note:* The hitter does not run out the first or second hit when runners are on base.
- *Rule:* At least one player must reach first base during the first round of hitting (9 batters). If no one reaches first, sides change, and the defensive team comes to bat. *Note:* This rule does not apply to Rounds 2, 3, or 4.
- Runners advance on errors, hits, walks, sacrifice flies, bunts, passed balls (third strike), wild pitches, catcher's interference, or when the pitcher hits the batter. *Note:* Do not allow intentional walks.
- A batter retires when he strikes out, fouls out, flies out, or grounds out on the third swing. He returns to the end of the line and hits in regular order.
- A player strikes out when he takes a third strike or fouls the third swing.
- A batter walks when the pitcher fails to throw a strike on 2 consecutive pitches.
- *Rule:* A hitter cannot advance beyond first base on extra base hits. For example, if the batter hits the

ball over the fence, he must stop at first. However, runners may score from second and third. A runner on first cannot go past third.

- Do not record the number of outs. Athletes continue to hit until sides change.
- The hitter receives 3 swings in his attempt to score runner(s). For example, the batter hits the first pitch for a single sending a runner to third. He has 2 more chances to knock in his teammate(s). If the hitter fails to score the runner(s), the runner(s) must leave the base, return to the line, and hit in regular order.
- If there are no runners on base and the batter hits the pitch, he must run the ball out.
- A runner may lead off base. He cannot steal.
- Each team hits for 2 rounds (optional). After 2 rounds, sides change. *Exception:* If no player reaches first base in the first round, sides change.

Time — One hour or more.

116. Three Pitch/Two Swing

Objective — To practice hitting, bunting, base running, and fielding.

Procedure — The procedure is as follows:

- The defensive team takes the field. The offensive team lines up near home plate.
- The batter receives 3 pitches. He gets 2 chances or 2 swings to hit the ball.
- The batter is free to bunt or swing away. If he hits the first pitch, he must run it out.
- An athlete strikes out when he swings through or fouls the second pitch, or takes the second pitch for a strike.
- A batter retires when he strikes out, fouls out, flies out, or grounds out. He returns to the line and hits in regular order.
- Runners advance on errors, hits, walks, sacrifice flies, bunts, passed balls (second strike), wild pitches, catcher's interference, or when the pitcher hits the batter. *Note:* Do not allow intentional walks.

- When a runner makes an out, he returns to the line, and hits in regular order.
- Runners, unless thrown out or tagged out, must remain on base until they score. Allow runners to steal.
- Each team bats for 10 minutes. After that time, runners clear the bases, and the offensive team takes the field. The defensive team comes to bat. Do not record the number of outs. Athletes continue to hit until sides change. Players keep their hitting order. For example, if the shortstop makes the last out, the left fielder bats when his team hits again. *Note:* Teams decide ahead of time which batting order to use.
- A round lasts approximately 20 minutes. The game consists of 3 rounds (optional).

Time — One hour and a half.

117. Split Hit

Objective — To practice hitting, bunting, base running, and fielding.
Procedure — The procedure is as follows:
- The defensive team takes the field. The offensive team lines up near home plate.
- The offensive team forms 2 lines. Five players go to Line A and 4 players go to Line B. Line A athletes act as hitters; they line up to the left of the batting cage. Line B players represent runners; they line up to the right of the batting cage. (Figure 69.)
- Action begins when Player 1, Line A, comes to bat. He has 2 chances or 2 swings to hit the ball. If he hits the ball into fair territory, Player 1, Line B, runs the ball out. If Player 1, Line B, makes an out, he goes to the end of Line A. Player 1, Line A, goes to the end of Line B.
- The hitter receives 2 swings. He may bunt or swing at the pitch. An athlete strikes out when he takes a second strike, fouls the ball on his second swing, or swings and misses on his second attempt.

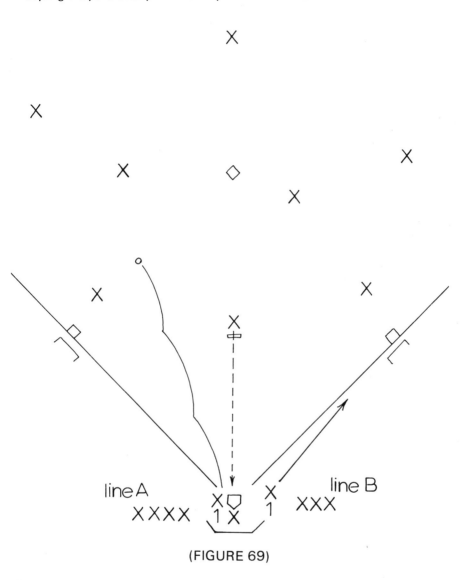

(FIGURE 69)

- A batter retires when he strikes out, pops out, flies out, or grounds out. He goes to Line B and becomes a runner.
- Runners advance on errors, hits, walks, sacrifice flies, bunts, passed balls (second strike), wild pitches, catcher's interference, or when the pitcher hits the batter. *Note:* Do not allow intentional walks. Allow runners to steal.

- A batter walks when the pitcher builds a three ball count. For example, the hurler runs a 2 ball, 1 strike count on the batter. If the pitcher's next delivery misses the strike zone, the batter walks.
- Each team bats for 15 minutes. After that time, runners clear the bases, and the offensive team takes the field. The defensive team comes to bat. Do not record the number of outs. Athletes continue to hit until sides change. Players keep their hitting order.
- A round lasts for 30 minutes. A round allows each team to field for 15 minutes and hit for 15 minutes. The game consists of 2 rounds (optional).

Time — One hour or more.

118. Alternate

Objective — To practice hitting, bunting, base running, and fielding.
Procedure — The procedure is as follows:

- The defensive team takes the field. The offensive team lines up near home plate. They bring a fungo bat and ball with them.
- Batters alternate swinging at the pitcher's delivery and hitting the ball with a fungo bat. For example, Batter 1 receives 2 swings to hit the pitched ball. If he hits the ball into fair territory, he runs it out. Batter 2 comes to home plate with fungo bat and ball. The hurler delivers a pitch to the catcher. When the pitch hits the catcher's mitt, the batter fungos his ball and runs it out. *Note:* The batter does not swing at the pitched ball. Play continues with Batter 3 hitting a live pitch, Batter 4 fungoing a ball, and so forth.
- Runners advance on errors, hits, walks, sacrifice flies, bunts, passed balls (first strike), wild pitches, catcher's interference, or when the pitcher hits the batter. *Note:* Do not allow stealing when a batter fungos the ball.
- The hitter may bunt the live pitch and fungo bunt the ball. *Rule:* A batter may fungo the ball between

the outfielders. He's not allowed to hit the ball over an outfielder's head.

- An athlete strikes out when he takes a second strike, fouls the ball on his second swing, or swings and misses on his second attempt. The fungo batter strikes out when he fouls the ball or swings and misses.
- A batter retires when he strikes out, fouls out, pops out, grounds out, or if he is a fungo batter hits the ball over an outfielder's head. He returns to the line and hits in regular order.
- A batter walks when the pitcher fails to throw a strike on 2 consecutive pitches.
- After 3 outs, runners clear the bases, return to the line, and hit in regular order.
- Each player hits 4 times (2 live/2 fungo) in one round before changing places with the defensive team. Regardless of number of outs, sides change. The game consists of 2 rounds (optional).

Time — One hour or more.

119. Single Swing Fungo

Objective — To practice base running, fielding, and hitting with the fungo bat.

Procedure — The procedure is as follows:

- The defensive team takes the field. The offensive team lines up near home plate. They keep a fungo bat and ball with them.
- Each batter, in turn, fungos a ball somewhere in the field. *Rule:* A batter is not allowed to hit a ball over an outfielder's head. If he does, he's out. However, the batter can place a ball between the outfielders.
- The athlete runs out every hit. A batter retires when he fouls the ball, swings and misses, grounds out, pops out, flies out, or hits the ball over an outfielder's head. He returns to the line and hits in regular order.
- Runners advance on errors, hits, sacrifice flies and bunts. They can lead off from base, but cannot steal.

- After 3 outs, runners clear the bases, return to the line, and hit in regular order.
- Each player hits 2 times in 1 round. After the last player hits, sides change. Players switch regardless of number of outs. The game consists of 3 rounds (optional).

Time — One hour or more.

120. Nine Tee

Objective — To practice base running, fielding, and hitting off the tee.

Procedure — The procedure is as follows:
- The defensive team takes the field. Use the pitcher and catcher as roving fielders. The pitcher, Rover 1, plays between left field and center field. The catcher, Rover 2, plays between center field and right field (Figure 70.) *Note:* The rover may play wherever he wishes within his area. The hitting team brings a batting tee and ball to home plate.
- Each batter, in turn, hits a ball off the tee. He runs out the ball.
- The defensive third baseman tells the batter how to set the tee, e.g., low inside corner, high outside corner, etc. The hitter must follow the baseman's direction. The defensive team adjusts accordingly. For example, if the batter (right-hander) sets the tee for a high outside pitch, fielders move to the right side of the diamond.
- A hitter retires when he fouls the ball, swings and misses, knocks the tee apart, grounds out, flies out, or pops out. He returns to the line and hits in regular order.
- A runner scores when he reaches third base safely. Players use home plate for hitting only.
- Runners advance on errors, hits, or sacrifice flies. *Note:* Do not allow runners to lead off or steal.
- After 3 outs, runners clear the bases, return to the line, and hit in regular order.
- Each player hits 2 times in 1 round. After the last

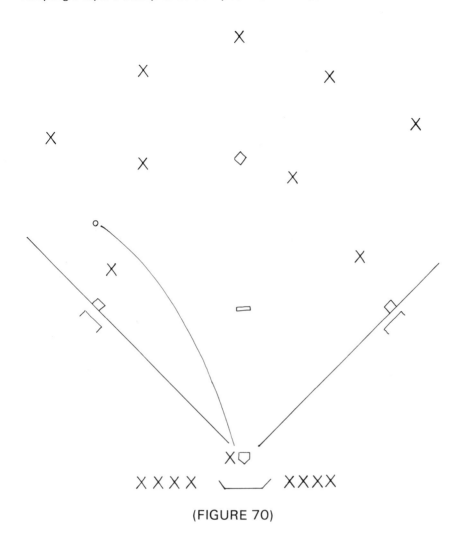

(FIGURE 70)

player hits, sides change. Players switch regardless of number of outs. The game consists of 3 rounds (optional).

Time — One hour or more.

121. Pop Toss

Objective — To practice hitting, bunting, base running, and fielding.
Procedure — The procedure is as follows:

- The defensive team takes the field. Use the pitcher as a roving fielder. He plays anywhere between the infield and outfield. The hitting team brings a ball to home plate. *Note:* Place a small net to the right of home plate. (Figure 71.) The net acts as a protective shield.
- Batters alternate tossing the ball and hitting the ball. Player 1, hitter, comes to home plate. Player 2, tosser, stands behind the net and tosses the ball over home plate.
- The batter receives 2 tosses or 2 chances to hit or bunt the ball into fair territory. If he hits a fair ball, he runs to first base. If he misses the ball or makes an out, he returns to the line. Player 2 also returns to the line. Action continues as Player 3 becomes hitter and Player 4 tosses the ball.
- A hitter retires when he strikes out (misses the last pitch), fouls the last pitch, grounds out, flies out, or pops out.
- If the tosser fails to throw a ball over home plate, the batter strikes out.
- Runners advance on hits, errors, sacrifice flies and bunts. *Note:* Do not allow players to lead off or steal.
- After 3 outs, runners clear the bases, return to the line, and hit or toss the ball.
- Each player hits and tosses the ball twice per round. After the last player hits, sides change. Players switch regardless of number of outs. The game consists of 3 rounds (optional).

Comment — The catcher stays behind third base. He's the only player allowed to tag runners at third. *Note:* A player scores when he reaches third safely. Home plate is used for hitting only.

Time — One hour or more.

122. One Pitch

Objective — To practice hitting, bunting, base running, and fielding.
Procedure — The procedure is as follows:

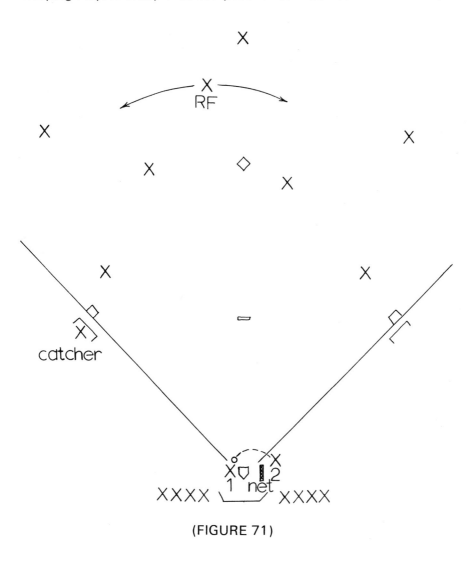

(FIGURE 71)

- The defensive team takes the field. The offensive team lines up near home plate.
- Each batter receives one pitch. If he hits the ball into fair territory, he runs to first base. If he makes an out, the batter returns to the line and hits in regular order.
- A hitter retires when he strikes out, grounds out, pops out, or flies out.
- Regular baseball rules apply. Runners advance on

hits, walks, errors, wild pitches, passed balls, sacrifice flies and bunts. *Note:* Do not allow intentional walks.
- Players can lead off from base and steal.
- A batter may bunt or swing away. A hitter strikes out when he swings and misses, or takes a called strike.
- The batter walks when the pitcher fails to throw a strike.
- After 3 outs, runners clear the bases, return to the line and hit in regular order.
- Each player hits 3 times in 1 round. After the last player hits, sides change. Players switch regardless of number of outs. The game consists of 3 rounds (optional).

Time — One hour or more.

123. Double Punch

Objective — To practice hitting, bunting, base running, and fielding.
Procedure — The procedure is as follows:
- Defensive players position themselves according to Figure 72. *Note:* This activity calls for 2 pitchers and 2 catchers. Pitcher 1 stands forward and to the left of the mound. Pitcher 2 stands forward and to the right of the mound. The batting cage protects each batter from line drives. Catchers stay approximately 60 feet from the pitchers. Rubber bases make suitable home plates. Three infielders and 2 outfielders spread around the diamond. The offensive team splits into 2 units, Station 1 and Station 2.
- Action begins when Batter 1, Station 1, comes to home plate. He receives 2 swings. If he hits the ball into fair territory, he runs it out. If he makes an out, he goes to the end of the line at Station 2. Batter 1, Station 2, comes to home plate. He follows the same procedure. If he makes an out, he goes to the end of the line at Station 1.
- When Pitcher 1 throws the ball, Pitcher 2 becomes

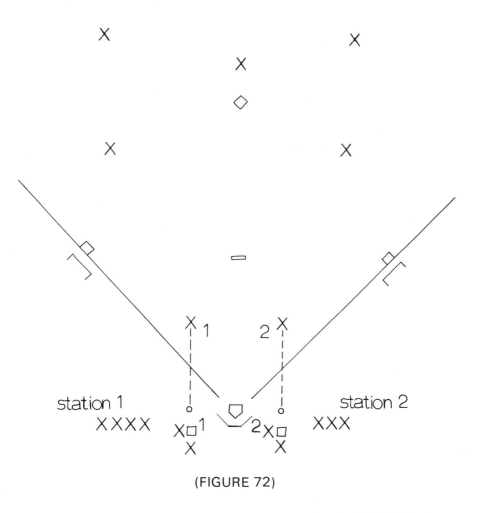

(FIGURE 72)

a fielder, and plays anywhere in the infield. Pitcher 1 becomes a fielder when Pitcher 2 throws the ball.

- Catcher 1 backs up all plays at third base; Catcher 2 backs up all plays at first base.
- The batter may bunt or swing away. He retires when he strikes out, flies out, pops out, or grounds out. A hitter strikes out when he misses the ball on his second swing or takes a second called strike. *Note:* Let only one hitter bat at a time.
- The batter walks when the pitcher misses the strike zone 2 times in succession.
- Runners advance on hits, errors, walks, passed

balls (second swing), wild pitches, or catcher's interference. *Note:* Do not allow intentional walks.
- Players can lead off from base, but cannot steal.
- A player scores a run when he reaches third base safely.
- After 3 outs, runners clear the bases, and go to the opposite stations.
- An athlete comes to bat 4 times in 1 round. After the last player hits, sides change. Players switch regardless of number of outs. The game consists of 2 rounds (optional).

Time — One hour or more.

124. Fun-Tee

Objective — To practice hitting, base running, and fielding.
Procedure — The procedure is as follows:
- The defensive team takes the field. The pitcher, Rover 1, plays behind the shortstop, between the left fielder and center fielder. The catcher, Rover 2, plays behind the second baseman, between the center fielder and right fielder. (Figure 73.) The offensive team brings a batting tee, ball, and fungo bat to home plate.
- Batters alternate hitting off the tee and hitting the ball with a fungo bat. For example, Batter 1 hits a ball off the tee; Batter 2 fungos the ball; Batter 3 hits off the tee; Batter 4 fungos the ball, and so on.
- If the batter hits the ball into fair territory, he runs it out. If he makes an out, he returns to the line, and hits in order.
- Runners advance on hits, errors, sacrifice flies, and bunts.
- A hitter may push bunt the ball off the tee or fungo bunt the ball. *Rule:* A batter may fungo the ball between the outfielders. He cannot hit it over their heads.
- The defensive third baseman tells the hitter how to set the batting tee, e.g., low inside corner, high out-side corner, etc. The hitter must follow the base-

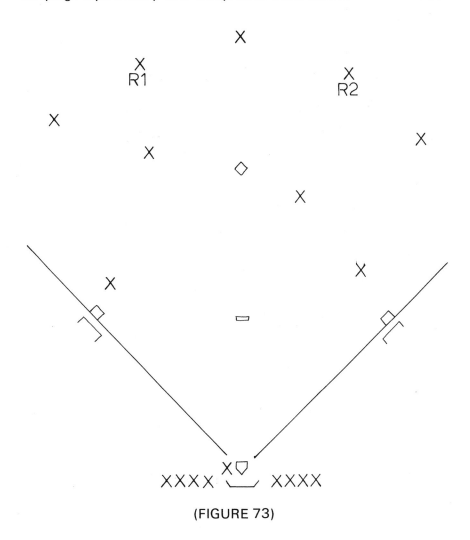

(FIGURE 73)

man's direction. The defensive team adjusts accordingly. For example, if the batter (right-hander) sets the tee for a high outside pitch, fielders move to the right side of the diamond.

- A batter retires when he strikes out, fouls out, grounds out, or if he is a fungo batter, hits the ball over an outfielder's head. He returns to the line and hits in regular order.
- An athlete strikes out when he swings and misses. A foul tip counts as a strike out.

- After 3 outs, runners clear the bases, return to the line, and hit in regular order.
- Each player hits 4 times (2 tee/2 fungo) in 1 round. After the last player hits, sides change. Players switch regardless of number of outs. The game consists of 2 rounds (optional).

Time — One hour or more.

8

Aggressive Sliding Drills and Games
for Every Player

The secret of sliding practice is to make it challenging, fun, and fast-moving. An effective sliding drill will test an athlete's speed, skill, thinking ability, and competitive spirit.

The activities in this unit emphasize the hook slide and bent-leg-and-go. *Note:* Before starting each drill, make sure fielders and runners wear protective equipment. Require a strong effort from every athlete. Warn runners not to slide at the last moment. A late slide can cause a serious leg or ankle injury.

125. Slide to the Side

Objective — To practice the hook slide.

Procedure — A catcher and pitcher take their positions. The coach stands to the shortstop side of second base. Players (runners) form a line near first base. (Figure 74.)

Action begins when a runner comes to first base. As the pitcher goes into a stretch, the runner takes his lead. *Note:* Before sliding practice, demonstrate how to lead off base, watch the pitcher's motion, and return to the base. If possible, cover these skills in preseason meeting.

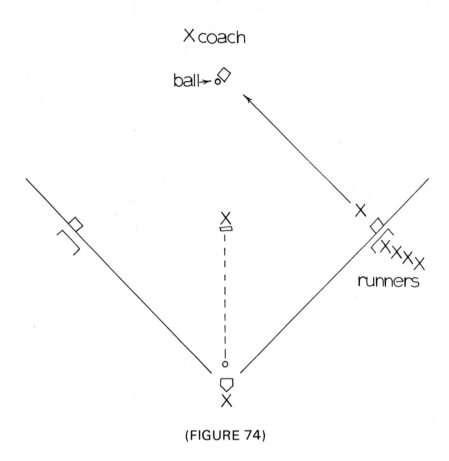

(FIGURE 74)

When the pitcher motions home, the runner breaks for second. The coach places a baseball on the inside corner or outside corner of second base. The runner slides to the opposite side of the ball.

Repeat several times. Replace the pitcher and catcher at intervals.

Comment — The coach is in excellent position to make corrections. Include these points when demonstrating the hook slide:

- The last foot to leave the ground is the one that tags the bag. For example, if the runner slides to the left, his left foot leaves the ground last.
- Keep body weight mostly on hip and to the sliding side of the bag.

- Slide directly into bag with hooked leg. Keep opposite leg extended and pointing away from the base. (Figure 75.)
- Move hands and elbows out of the way.
- When toe hits bag, tighten and hold.
- Slide away from the fielder. Force him to reach out and make the tag.

Time — 20 minutes.

(FIGURE 75)

126. Slide Side Around

Objective — To practice the hook slide.

Procedure — Three athletes bring a ball with them to the field. Player 1 stands to the shortstop side of second base; Player 2 stays to the left of third base; Player 3 stands behind home plate. The coach and players (runners) stay near first base. (Figure 76.) A runner comes to first base.

Action begins when the coach yells "Go" and the runner breaks for second. Player 1 sets a ball to one side of the bag. The runner slides to the opposite side of the ball. Play continues as the runner slides into third base and home plate. Players 2 and 3 follow the same procedure as Player 1. After each slide, the

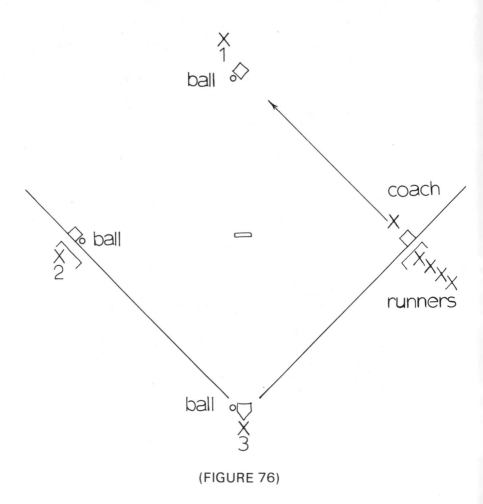

(FIGURE 76)

runner takes his lead, and breaks when the coach hollers "Go."

Athletes rotate in this manner: Runner becomes Player 1, Player 1 becomes Player 2, Player 2 becomes Player 3, and Player 3 goes to the end of the line.

Comment — Repeat 2 or 3 times.
Time — 20 to 25 minutes.

127. Coach Approach

Objective — To practice the hook slide.
Procedure — A catcher, pitcher, second baseman, shortstop, and

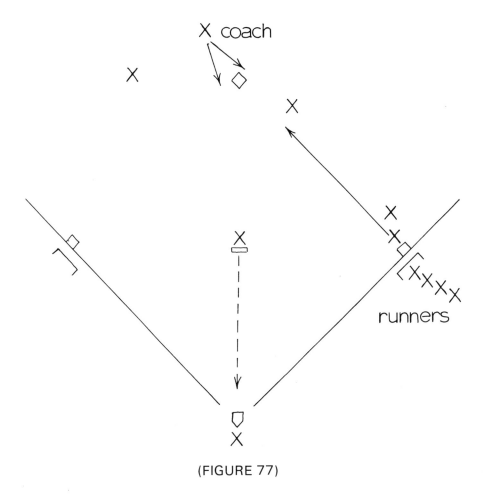

(FIGURE 77)

first baseman take the field. The coach stands to the shortstop side of second base. Runners line up near first base. (Figure 77.)

Action begins when a runner comes to first base. As the pitcher goes into a stretch, the runner takes his lead. When the pitcher motions home, the runner breaks for second. The catcher makes a throw to second. The coach, watching the throw, points to the side of the bag he wants the runner to slide. *Note:* Make sure the runner has plenty of time to prepare for his slide.

Set up a contest. Let the BR's, base runners,

compete against the F's, fielders. The coach, acting as umpire, awards points as follows:

Points	For	If
2	BR's	Runner is safe at second.
2	F's	Second baseman or shortstop tags out runner.

Have losing side pay with push-ups or laps.

Comment — Repeat several times. Change fielders at intervals. Have the second baseman and shortstop take turns making the tag and backing up the throw. Tell the fielder to let the runner tag himself out. The pitcher should keep runners honest by occasionally throwing to first.

Time — 20 to 25 minutes

128. Second and Home

Objective — To practice the hook slide.

Procedure — A catcher, pitcher, second baseman, shortstop, and first baseman take the field. The coach stands between the pitcher's mound and second base. Runners line up near first base.

Action begins when a runner comes to first base. As the pitcher goes into a stretch, the runner takes his lead. The coach calls out "Left, Right," "Left, Left," "Right, Left," or "Right, Right." The runner must slide into second base and home plate. The called direction tells the player which side of the base to slide. For example, "Left, Right" means hook slide to the left of second and hook slide to the right of home plate.

After a runner slides into second, action stops. Fielders return to their positions and the runner leads from second. When the pitcher motions home, the runner breaks for third. As the runner approaches third, the catcher throws to second base. The second baseman or shortstop throws home to get the runner.

Set up a contest. Let the BR's (base runners)

compete against the F's (fielders). The coach, acting as umpire, awards points as follows:

Points	For	If
2	BR's	Runner is safe at second or home.
2	F's	Second baseman, shortstop or catcher tags out runner.

Have losing side pay with push-ups or laps.

Comment — Tell the catcher and fielders to keep their throws to the opposite side of the slide. For example, on a "Left, Right" call, the catcher throws to the right of second and the fielder throws to the left of home plate. *Suggestion:* Instruct the catcher on proper plate coverage.

Time — 25 to 30 minutes.

129. Sliding Game One

Objective — To practice the hook slide.

Procedure — A pitcher, shortstop, second baseman, first baseman, and catcher take the field. Players (runners) line up near first base. The coach stands to the shortstop side of second base. He watches play and makes corrections.

Action begins when a runner comes to first base. As the pitcher goes into a stretch, the runner takes his lead. After the ball hits the catcher's mitt, the runner breaks for second. The catcher tosses the ball to the left, to the right, or in front of the pitcher's mound. (Figure 78.) The pitcher fields and throws to second. The shortstop and second baseman take turns fielding and backing up the play. Play continues as the runner returns to the end of the line.

Set up a contest. Award points as suggested in Drill 127: *Coach Approach.*

Comment — Here are some suggestions for fielders:
- Let fielders and runners trade off at intervals.
- Have the pitcher hold runners close to the base.

- Tell the catcher to adjust his tosses to keep plays close at second.

Time — 20 to 25 minutes.

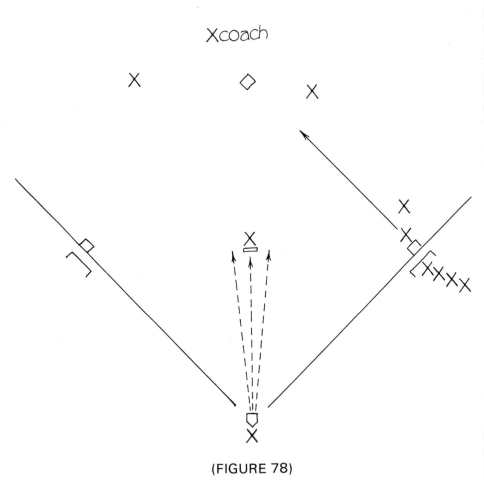

(FIGURE 78)

130. Sliding Game Two

Objective — To practice the hook slide.

Procedure — Infielders, including pitcher, take the field. Players (runners) line up near first base. The coach sets a baseball between the mound and third base. He stands behind second base to watch play and make corrections. (Figure 79.)

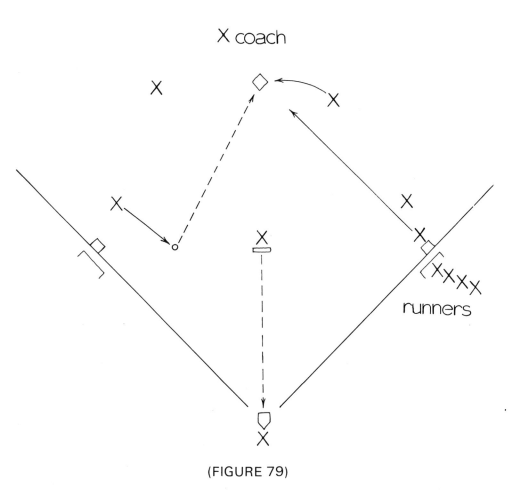

(FIGURE 79)

Action begins when a runner comes to first base. As the pitcher goes into a stretch, the runner takes his lead. After the ball hits the catcher's mitt, the runner breaks for second. The third baseman fields the placed ball and throws to second. After the play, the runner replaces the ball and goes to the end of the line. The next runner comes to first, leads off, and breaks for second. The pitcher fields the placed ball and throws to second. The runner replaces the ball and goes to the end of the line. Play continues with the third baseman and pitcher taking turns fielding and throwing.

Set up a contest. Award points as suggested in Drill 127: *Coach Approach.*

Comment — Have fielders and runners trade off at intervals. Let the shortstop and second baseman take turns tagging the runner.

Time — 20 to 25 minutes.

131. Sliding Game Three

Objective — To practice the hook slide.

Procedure — Same as Drill 130: *Sliding Game Two,* with these exceptions:
- The coach sets a baseball (Ball 1) between third base, shortstop, and pitcher's mound. He places a second ball (Ball 2) near the first base line between home plate and pitcher's mound.
- The third baseman and pitcher take turns fielding and throwing Ball 1. The first baseman, catcher, and pitcher take turns fielding and throwing Ball 2.

Comment — See Drill 130: *Sliding Game Two.*

Time — 20 to 25 minutes.

132. Pop and Stop Game

Objective — To practice the hook slide.

Procedure — Divide athletes into 3 groups, 6 players per group. Group 1, batters, go to home plate; Group 2, fielders, take the infield; Group 3, runners, line up near first base. (Figure 80.) *Note:* Keep extra players busy (coaching bases, etc.) until they enter the game. The coach, acting as umpire, stands behind the pitcher.

Action begins when a runner goes to first base and a batter comes to home plate. The batter, using a choke grip, attempts to score the runner. He can bunt or hit. A runner scores when he slides safely into second, third, and home. After the runner scores or makes an out, another batter comes to the plate, and the retired batter goes to the end of the line.

Here are rules for runners:
- Hook slide into second base, third base, and home plate.

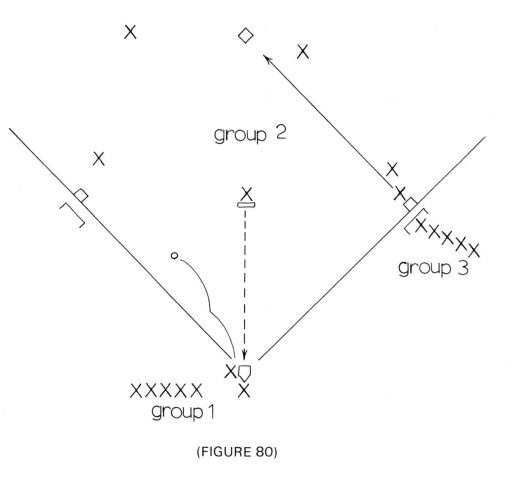

(FIGURE 80)

- Do not break from the base until the batter hits the ball.
- Test the pitcher's move. Take a good lead. *Note:* If the runner gets picked off, he leaves the base and goes to the end of the line. Another runner takes his place. However, the batter stays at home plate.
- Do not steal or advance on a passed ball.
- Advance only one base at a time. *Exception:* Take an extra base on fielding and throwing errors.
- If the runner is tagged out, he returns to the end of the line.

Here are rules for batters:

- A batter loses his turn if he fails to hit the ball on

two attempts, e.g., fouls the pitches or swings and misses.

- A batter loses his turn if he hits the ball over an infielder's head. *Exceptions:* (1) If an infielder, say third baseman, runs toward the plate to field a bunt; (2) If a ball goes over the pitcher's head.

    Have Groups 1 and 3 challenge Group 2. Group 2 players receive 1 point each time a runner or batter makes an out; Groups 1 and 3 receive 3 points each time a runner scores. The losing team pays with push-ups or laps.

Comment — Have pitchers throw straight balls at three-quarters speed. Emphasize the importance of control. Place athletes in the group where they need the most help. Assign players who need extra sliding practice to Group 3.

Time — 25 to 30 minutes.

133. Burst From Third

Objective — To practice the hook slide.
Procedure — The same as Drill 132: *Pop and Stop Game,* with these exceptions:
- Group 3 players line up near third base.
- A runner scores when he slides safely into home plate.
- After the runner scores or makes an out, he goes to Group 1; the batter goes to Group 3.
- A batter loses his turn if he fails to hit the ball on his first attempt.

Comment — See Drill 132: *Pop and Stop Game.*
Time — 20 minutes.

134. Dummy Pop Game

Objective — To practice the hook slide.
Procedure — Players line up near first base. The coach brings a tape measure and football tackling dummy to second base. He stands to the right of second and holds the dummy upright on the base.

Action begins when a runner comes to first base. He leads off from first base. When the coach yells "Go," the runner breaks for second and hook slides into the dummy.

Have the manager come to second base and record the distance each player knocks the dummy from second base. (see chart) Give each player 5 tries. The player with the highest total distance wins.

Recording Chart

Player	1	2	3	4	5	Total Distance

Comment — Don't spend too much time taking measurements. Keep athletes constantly on the move.

Time — 20 to 25 minutes.

135. Fungo Slide Game

Objective — To practice the hook slide and bent-leg-and-go.

Procedure — Infielders, excluding pitcher, take the field. Players (runners) line up near first base. The coach brings a fungo bat and ball to home plate.

Action begins when a runner comes to first base and takes a lead. When the coach hollers "Go," the runner breaks for second. He slides into second with a bent-leg-and-go, returns to his feet, and heads for third. As the runner touches third, the coach fungos a ground ball to an infielder. The infielder throws to the catcher. The runner hook slides into home plate. Play continues with the next runner coming to first base.

Set up a contest. Award points as suggested in Drill 127: *Coach Approach.*

Comment — Demonstrate the bent-leg-and-go slide. Give players these points:
- Extend the first foot to leave the ground in front of the body.
- Bend the take-off foot under the knee of the extended leg.
- The body assumes a sit-down position with the extended leg pointing over the base. (Figure 81.)

(FIGURE 81)

- Body momentum and a push from the bent leg or ground brings the slider to his feet. This happens before the slide is completed.
- The extended foot hits the bag and helps carry the runner forward.
- Pushing off the bent leg and extended foot throws the runner in a forward motion.

Time — 20 to 25 minutes.

136.   Bent-Leg-and-Go Sprint

Objective — To practice the bent-leg-and-go slide.
Procedure — Players line up to the right of home plate. The coach, standing to the left of the line, times each player around the bases.

Action begins when a runner comes to home plate. When the coach yells "Go," the runner takes off around the bases. He slides into first, second, and third. After sliding into third, he sprints for home plate. The runner does not slide into home plate. Let players run two times around the bases. Record times on a chart.
Comment — Keep times posted on the gymnasium office wall. Encourage athletes to improve their times.
Time — 15 to 20 minutes.

137.   Bases Full

Objective — To practice the hook slide and bent-leg-and-go slide.
Procedure — Players (runners) divide into 3 groups. Group 1 stands near first base; Group 2 stays near second base; Group 3 goes to third base. The coach remains near home plate. A runner from each group goes to his base.

When the coach hollers "Go," runners take off. They run the following pattern:

Group 1 Runner — Bent-leg-and-go into second, bent-leg-and-go into third, hook slides into home, and sprints to first.

Group 2 Runner — Bent-leg-and-go into third, hook slides into home, bent-leg-and-go into first, and sprints to second.

Group 3 Runner — Hook slides into home, bent-leg-and-go into first, bent-leg-and-go into second, and sprints to third.

After runners complete the circuit, they rotate. Group 1 runner goes to Group 2; Group 2 runner goes to Group 3; Group 3 runner goes to Group 1.
Comment — Have each player run the bases 2 or 3 times. Tell athletes to keep moving. Avoid pile ups on the bases.
Time — 20 minutes.

Make sliding an important part of practice. Tell players a good slider stays low, hits hard, and gives a one hundred per cent effort.

Allow athletes sufficient time to warm up. Include plenty of stretching and bending exercises.

9

Employing Indoor Drills and Games During Inclement Weather

Rain dampens many things including baseball schedules, fields, and players' spirit. However, inclement weather needn't put you behind your opponent.

This unit provides the coach with handy drills and games that stress conditioning, throwing, fielding, bunting, and batting skills within the confines of the gym.

138. Up and Back

Objective — To strengthen the legs.
Procedure — Divide the players into 4 teams, 6 players per group (optional). Try to keep teams evenly balanced. Teams pair off and separate. Place a ball and glove about 50 feet in front of Line 1. Set an empty glove approximately 50 feet in front of Line 2. The coach stands near Group A; another player or manager stands near Group B. (Figure 82.) They record the time it takes each group to complete the drill.

Action begins when the coach yells "Go." The first player in Line 1 from each group runs to the glove, picks up the ball, runs to the second glove, places the ball in the pocket, sprints to Line 2, tags the first

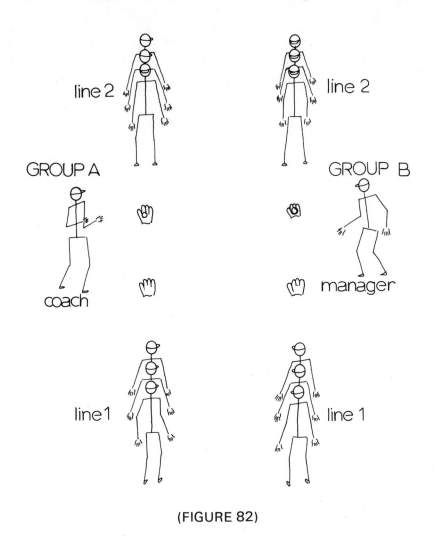

(FIGURE 82)

player, and goes to the end of the line. The tagged
player runs to the glove, picks up the ball, runs to the
second glove, places the ball in the pocket, sprints to
Line 1, tags the first player, and goes to the end of the
line. When every player runs the circuit, action stops,
and the time is recorded. Play continues for 5 more
rounds.

Add a competitive factor. Call out the time for
each round. Tell players they must improve their times

with each successive run or start over again with round one.

Comment — Advise athletes against hedging. Assign a penalty to those players taking it easy.

Time — 15 to 20 minutes.

139. Push Up Away

Objective — To offer a competitive conditioning drill.

Procedure — Divide team into 4 equal lines. Keep lines approximately 30 feet apart. Set a baseball in a glove about 100 feet in front of each line. (Figure 83.)

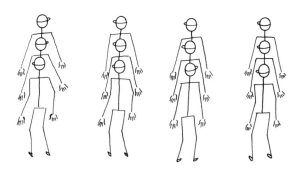

(FIGURE 83)

On command "Go," the first player in each line sprints to the glove, does 5 push-ups, picks up the ball, runs back to the line, and does 5 more push-ups. After completing the last push-up, the runner hands the ball to the next player, and goes to the end of the line. The player sprints to the glove, replaces the ball, does 5 push-ups, picks up the ball, runs back to the line, does 5 more push-ups, gives the ball to the next player, and goes to the end of the line. Play continues with each player running the circuit 3 times. The first team to finish wins.

Comment — Convince athletes that honesty pays. Award 5 extra push-ups to players who miscount.

Time — 10 minutes.

140. Figure Four

Objective — To practice making accurate throws.

Procedure — Divide the team into groups, 4 players per group. Position groups around the gym. Players (with gloves) form a square and stay about 60 feet apart. A ball rests in the center of the square. (Figure 84.)

Action begins when Player 1 runs to the ball, picks it up, throws to Player 2, and returns to his position. The ball goes around the horn twice. The

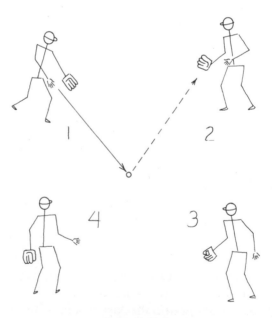

(FIGURE 84)

second time Player 1 catches the ball, he runs to the center of the square, replaces the ball, and returns to his position. Action continues with Player 2 fielding and throwing to Player 3, and so on.

Comment — Go as many rounds as time permits. Have athletes concentrate on making accurate throws. If the gym becomes congested, use soft rubber balls to prevent injuries from wild throws.

Time — 10 to 15 minutes.

141. Time Around

Objective — To offer a competitive conditioning drill.

Procedure — Set up an indoor baseball diamond with rubber bases 90 feet apart. Players line up near home plate. The coach, holding a timer, stands near home plate.

Action begins when a player brings a bat to home plate. He takes his normal batting stance. On "Go," the player swings the bat and runs the bases. The coach records the time for each player on a chart.

Comment — End the practice session with *Time Around.* Keep times posted on the gym wall. Advise athletes to improve their times by practicing proper base running techniques. *Note:* Show players how to circle the bases. Have them trot around the bases 2 or 3 times prior to the drill.

Time — 10 to 15 minutes.

142. Stop and Stoop

Objective — To combine running and bending exercises.

Procedure — Divide the players into 2 equal groups, A and B. Each group splits into 2 even teams. The 2 teams in each group separate and form a line 90 to 100 feet apart.

Tape 3 zones, 6 inches square, equidistant between Groups A and B. Place a tennis ball or soft rubber ball in each square. (Figure 85.)

Play begins when the coach yells "Go." The first man in each line, Player A, runs to each square, picks up the balls, and circles Group B. On his way back to

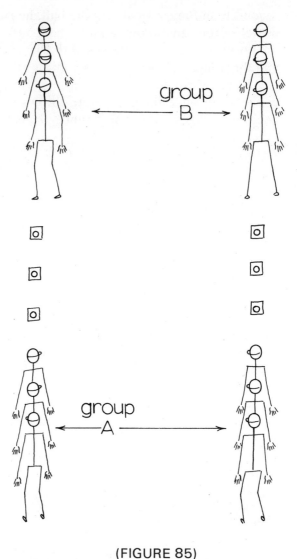

(FIGURE 85)

Group A, he replaces each ball, and runs to the end of the line. The first athlete in Group B takes off when Player A reaches the end of the line. Player B repeats the same procedure.

Action continues for 2 rounds (optional). Each player runs the course two times. If a player drops a ball, he must pick it up. No other player can interfere.

If a ball rolls out of the taped square, the running player must replace it.

The coach acts as judge. If he catches players running out of turn, breaking too soon, or interfering, he assigns a penalty to the erring team.

Comment — Have the losing team put equipment away after practice. The competitive atmosphere keeps the adrenalin, and perspiration, flowing.

Time — 10 to 15 minutes.

143. Spin Around Game

Objective — To practice making accurate throws.

Procedure — Divide team into groups of 3 players. Keep teams far enough apart to avoid collisions. Player 1 and Player 2 stand about 20 feet apart. Player 1 has his back turned to Player 2. Player 3 stays approximately 90 feet from Player 2. (Figure 86.)

Athletes compete against each other. Action begins when Player 2 bounces a soft rubber ball against the floor and yells "Turn." Player 1 spins around, fields, and throws to Player 3. Player 3 returns the ball to Player 2. Each player receives 3 turns to field and throw. After the third play, athletes rotate. Player 1 becomes Player 3, Player 3 becomes Player 2, and Player 2 becomes Player 1. Go as many rounds as time permits.

Comment — Have athletes keep their own scores. Award 1 point for clean fielding and 1 point for accurate throws. The player with the most points after 2 rounds wins.

Time — 15 to 20 minutes.

144. Situation Game*

Objective — To play an indoor baseball game.

Procedure — Set up a baseball diamond with bases 60 feet apart. Select 2 teams, 9 players per team.

---

*Hoehn, Robert G., Thomas J. Rowen Booklet Service, *Indoor Baseball Games and Drills,* Santa Clara, CA., 1974, pp. 41-44.

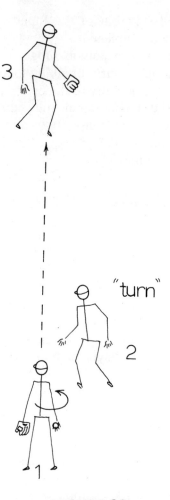

(FIGURE 86)

Play begins when the defense, Team A, takes the field. The catcher wears full protective equipment, e.g., chest protector, face mask, shin guards, and supporter. The offense, Team B, sends a man to first base. A batter comes to home plate. He receives 3 pitches. Each pitch presents a different situation. They are as follows:

Situation One, First Pitch — The batter has a 3-1 count; he must hit-and-run.

Situation Two, Second Pitch — The hitter must bunt.

Situation Three, Third Pitch — The hitter can bunt or swing away. *Note:* Batters should use a smooth, easy swing with a complete follow-through. Hitters run out the last swing.

Game rules are as follows:

- A batter makes an out if he swings and misses a pitch, fouls a pitch, or takes a called strike.
- He reaches base on walks (pitcher misses on all 3 deliveries), catcher's interference, errors, being hit by the pitch, or base hits. The batter runs out only the third pitch. However, runners go every time the batter hits the ball.
- Runners advance on base hits, errors, wild pitches, tag ups, or passed balls. Do not allow stealing. Exception: Hit-and-run.
- Every player bats twice each inning. The pitcher throws a soft rubber ball 18 times. *Note:* If you don't want your pitcher throwing a light ball, use another player.
- After 3 outs, runners leave the bases and return to the end of the line. Another player goes to first base, and play continues. After every hitter bats twice, sides change regardless of number of outs. Team B takes the field; Team A comes to bat.
- The catcher (designated player or coach) umpires the game.
- Advise pitchers to throw half speed; warn runners not to slide or interfere with play.
- The team scoring the most runs wins.

Comment — Have extra players coach the bases. To make the drill more effective, you may wish to demonstrate any of these skills:

- Hitting behind the runner.
- Proper bunting techniques.
- Rundowns.
- Hitting up the middle of the diamond.
- Base running tips, e.g., leading off base, getting a good jump, etc.

Advise players to swing easy and make solid contact with the ball.

Time — 45 minutes to one hour.

145. Six Inning Bunt Game*

Objective — To play an indoor baseball game.

Procedure — Set up a baseball diamond with bases 60 feet apart. Select 2 teams, 6 players per team.

Play begins when the defense, Team A, takes the field. The offense, Team B, sends a man to first base. A batter comes to home plate. It's his job to advance the runner.

Game rules are as follows:

- The batter receives 2 pitches. He must bunt. Every player bats 2 times each inning.
- If the batter fails to bunt the ball into fair territory, he's out, and returns to the end of the line.
- The hurler throws a soft rubber ball at half speed 12 times. *Note:* If you don't want your pitcher throwing a light ball, use another player.
- If the pitcher fails to throw strikes or hits the batter, the batter is awarded first base. The next man in line comes to the plate.
- After 3 outs, runners leave the bases and return to the end of the line. After every hitter bats twice, sides change regardless of number of outs. Team B takes the field; Team A comes to bat.
- Runners advance on walks, tag ups, wild pitches, passed balls, errors, bunts, or steals — if it's part of offensive strategy.
- Runners leave the bases after 3 outs. Another player goes to first base, and play continues. Caution runners not to slide or interfere with play.
- The catcher (designated player or coach) umpires the game. *Note:* Make sure catchers wear full protective gear.
- Keep the game going for six innings. Make substitutions at intervals. Try to include as many players as possible.
- The team scoring the most runs in six innings wins. Award extra laps or push-ups to the losing side.

Ibid, p. 38-41.

Comment — The offensive team, by prearranged signals, can execute plays, e.g., suicide or safety squeeze, run and bunt, fake bunt and run, etc.

Infielders have an opportunity to practice defensive strategy, e.g., base coverage, force outs, rundowns, stopping the squeeze play, and so on.

Keep players busy and have athletes play their normal positions. Extra players can work individual or small group drills until the coach calls for them.

Time — 45 minutes to one hour.

146. Bunt Back Game

Objective — To practice bunting the ball.

Procedure — Divide team into groups of 6 to 8 players. Keep teams far enough apart to avoid collisions. Group A, bunters, and Group B, pitchers, stand about 90 feet apart. (Figure 87.)

Action begins when a Group B player pitches a soft rubber ball to a Group A player. Player A bunts the ball to the left or to the right of the pitcher. The pitcher fields and throws the ball to the man directly behind him. After 3 bunts, the bunter goes to Group B; pitcher goes to Group A. The next players in line become pitcher and bunter respectively.

Award one point for each properly bunted ball. The player with the most points after 3 rounds wins.

Comment — Use old rags or towels for base lines. Have batters concentrate on bunting balls near the base lines. Prior to the drill, demonstrate how to properly bunt the ball. Tell pitchers to throw strikes at one half speed.

Time — 20 to 25 minutes.

147. Six Outs

Objective — To practice bunting and fielding.

Procedure — Divide athletes into 4 groups, 5 players per group (optional). Set up 2 baseball diamonds, bases 60 feet apart, near the gym wall. Group A, hitters, gather

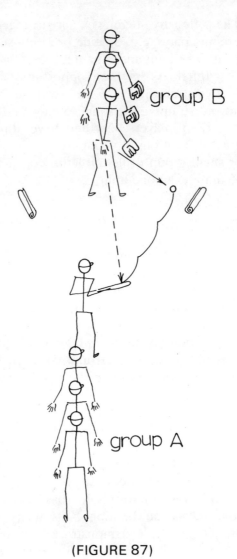

group B

group A

(FIGURE 87)

near home plate; Group B, fielders, position themselves according to Figure 88.

Action begins when a hitter comes to home plate. The pitcher throws a soft rubber ball at half speed to the catcher. *Note:* If you don't want your pitcher throwing a light ball, use another player.

Rules are as follows:

• The batter receives one chance to bunt. He may

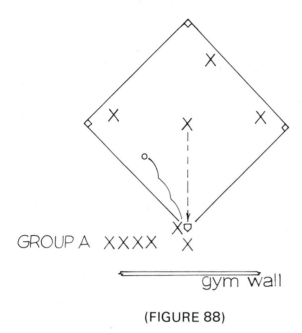

GROUP A XXXX X

gym wall

(FIGURE 88)

bunt any way he wishes. *Note:* Urge teams to use prearranged signals for safety and suicide squeeze plays.
- The batter must run out every hit. If he fouls or misses the pitch, he's out, and returns to the line.
- Batters must hit in turn.
- Fielders are not allowed to leave their positions until the batter bunts the ball.
- After 6 outs, players change sides.
- Each team keeps its own score.
- Continue play as long as time permits.

Comment — Try to have athletes play their normal positions. Advise pitchers to work on control. Wild pitching slows down play and creates confusion. Make sure catchers wear full protective gear.

Time — 45 minutes to one hour.

148. Double or Nothing

Objective — To practice hitting, running, fielding, and throwing.

Procedure — Divide athletes into 4 groups, 5 players per group (optional). Set up 2 baseball diamonds, bases 60 feet apart. Group A, hitters, gather near home plate; Group B, fielders, position themselves according to Figure 89. Catchers wear full protective gear.

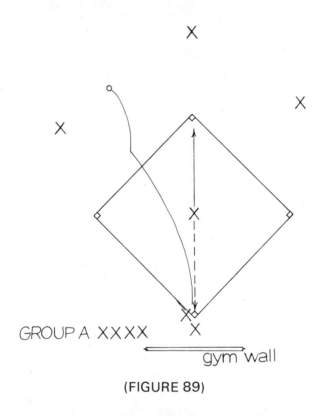

GROUP A XXXX

gym wall

(FIGURE 89)

Action begins when a hitter comes to home plate. The pitcher throws a soft rubber ball at half speed. *Note:* If you don't want your pitcher to throw a light ball, use another player.

Rules are as follows:
- The batter receives 2 swings. He must reach second base safely on his hit.
- A batter makes an out when he: (a) Misses the second pitch; (b) Pops up or fouls the ball; (c) Fails to reach second base; (d) Hits the ball over a fielder's head.

- A runner must stay on base until the batter hits the ball. He cannot lead off, steal, or slide into base.
- The pitcher covers second base; fielders back up each other and make accurate throws to second or home.
- A runner on second must score when the batter hits the ball. If he fails to score, he's out, and returns to the line.
- After 6 outs, players change sides.
- Each team keeps its own score.
- Continue play as long as time permits.

Comment — Keep players moving on and off the field. Remind pitchers that control is the key to successful play.

Time — 45 minutes to one hour.

149. Two Strikes

Objective — To give players actual game situations.

Procedure — Set up a baseball diamond with bases 60 feet apart. Select 2 teams, 9 players per team. Keep players at their regular positions.

Action begins when an offensive player comes to bat. Regular baseball rules apply with these exceptions:

- Batters must use a choke grip and swing for base hits. Hard swinging is not allowed.
- A batter receives 2 strikes. He may bunt or swing away.
- No leading off, stealing, or sliding.
- The pitcher throws a soft rubber ball at half speed. *Note:* If you don't want your pitcher throwing a light ball, use another player.
- The coach, standing behind the pitcher's mound, umpires the game.
- After 3 outs, sides change.
- The coach keeps score. He assigns laps or push-ups to the losing team.
- Continue play as long as time permits.

Comment — Keep extra players busy coaching bases or working in small groups. Make sure catchers wear full protective gear.

Time — One hour or more.

150. One Hop Stop

Objective — To give players actual game situations.
Procedure — Follow the same procedure described in Drill 149: *Two Strikes,* with one exception: The pitcher throws a single bouncer to the hitter, e.g., he bounces the ball up to the plate.
Comment — See Comment, Drill 149.
Time — One hour or more.

How To Set Up An Indoor Practice

A successful indoor practice session hinges on three things: (1) Organization; (2) Handling of personnel; (3) Facilities. Let's take these items one at a time.

Organization

Expect cold, rainy weather to chase your practice indoors. Be ready to work out inside the gym. The following program will act as a guide.

TEAM MEETING (15 to 20 minutes)
Go over the day's activities. Give each player his assignment. Make sure athletes know what is expected of them. Introduce drills or demonstrate the fundamentals to be stressed for that day.

WARM UP (25 to 30 minutes)
Jog 5 or 6 times around the gym. Do plenty of bending and stretching exercises. Players pair off and throw for approximately 15 minutes.

SMALL GROUP WORK (20 to 25 minutes)
Separate into small groups. Pitchers and catchers pair off. Pitchers throw from one half to three-quarters speed. They work from the stretch and wind-up, combining fast balls, curves, and change ups.

Infielders and outfielders play pepper, work small group drills (See Chapter 3: *Employing Fast-Moving Drills for Small Groups*), or do pick-ups.

TEAM DRILLS (45 to 60 minutes)
Use Drills 144, 145, 146, 147, 148, 149, or 150. Have extra players work in small groups, swing a weighted bat, hit off a batting tee, etc., until they enter the drill.

END OF PRACTICE (15 to 20 minutes)

Finish practice with competitive running drills. Use Drills 138, 139, 141, or 142. Have pitchers run wind sprints or do pick-ups.

Handling of personnel

Each player should have a thorough understanding of policies and procedures. He should know where he stands at all times. Practice sessions run smoother when players know what is expected of them and a good time to spell out these guidelines is early in the season. The following rules are extremely important:

- Be ready to practice — rain or shine. The best way to build hard feelings is to say, "It's raining. Nobody practices on rainy days!".
- Be on time for practice. Don't keep us guessing.
- Have a good reason for missing practice. You owe it to yourself, your teammates, and your coach. Flimsy excuses won't make it here.
- If you must miss practice, tell the coach ahead of time. Don't wait until the last minute. We don't like surprises.
- If in doubt about practice, check with the coach. Don't rely on the word of someone else.

Facilities

The coach makes plans according to the availability of space. Rainy days may find the track team, tennis team, and golf team invading the gym. What does a coach do with limited space? He must decide which players need the most work (usually pitchers and catchers).

The following considerations will make the coach's job easier:

- Sign up for the gym early in the year. Tempers flare when teams make a last minute dash for the gym.
- Confer with fellow coaches. Work out an agreement to everyone's satisfaction.
- Check with district policy. Some schools frown on throwing baseballs inside the gym.
- Protect school equipment and facilities. Cover breakable items with mats or pads.
- Begin and end practice on time. Don't cut into another coach's plans.

10

Drills for Players with Fielding, Throwing, and Hitting Problems

Fielding, throwing, and hitting problems persist throughout the season. Some athletes need special help and extra practice time to overcome their problems. This unit serves as an extension of Chapters 4, 5, and 6.

Fielding Problems

151. High Sun

Objective — To give players practice catching fly balls in the sun.
Procedure — The coach and back-up man stand with their backs to the sun. Players gather in the field. The coach hits towering fly balls into the sun. Players take turns fielding and throwing to the back-up man.
Comment — Tell athletes to use their bare hands or gloves to shield the sun from their eyes.
Time — 15 to 20 minutes.

152. Turning the Head

Objective — To keep from turning the head when fielding ground balls.

Procedure — The coach and back-up man stand near the back-stop or side line fence. Players spread out and stay about 100 feet away from the coach.

Action begins with the coach hitting soft ground balls to each player. Athletes field and throw to the back-up man. When the coach hollers "Move," athletes step 10 feet closer to the coach. As the players move closer, the coach hits the ball harder. Action continues until players are approximately 50 feet from the coach.

Comment — Have players stay low, keep weight forward, and fix eyes on the ball. Tell them to look the ball into the glove and use the bare hand to cover the ball after it hits the glove.

Time — 20 to 25 minutes.

153. Fielding First Baseman

Objective — To give the first baseman fielding practice.

Procedure — The first baseman stands by a rubber base placed near a side line fence. The coach and back-up man stay about 60 feet from the base. The coach tosses low, bouncing balls at different angles. The baseman shifts his feet according to the throw.

Comment — Keep the baseman moving to his left and to his right. Mix low and high throws. Watch the baseman's feet as he shifts from side to side. Check to see that his extended foot doesn't pull his back foot off the base.

Time — 10 to 15 minutes.

154. Right and Left

Objective — To practice fielding to the right and to the left.

Procedure — Place 6 baseballs 50 feet apart according to Figure 90. The coach and back-up man stand about 90 feet away from the fielder.

Action begins when the coach yells "Go." The fielder breaks to his left, picks up the ball, and throws to the back-up man. He then breaks right, picks up the ball, and throws to the back-up man. Play continues

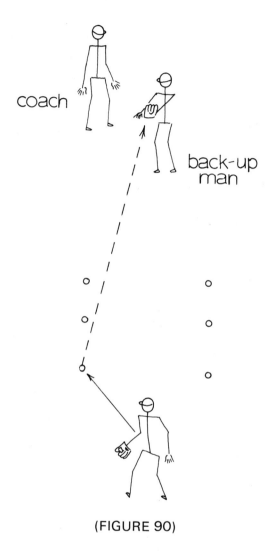

coach

back-up
man

(FIGURE 90)

with the athlete moving left to right until he fields all
6 balls. Repeat 2 or 3 times.

Comment — Tell fielders to stay low and move quickly to the ball.
When running to the right, have fielder stop in front
of ball, set right foot against the ground, and throw
using the right foot for support. When running to the
left, have fielder come up throwing off the right foot
while pointing left foot in the direction of the throw.

Time — 10 to 15 minutes.

Throwing Problems

155. Accurate Throw

Objective — To help players build speed and accuracy in throwing.
Procedure — Place 5 baseballs in a straight line about 30 feet apart. The coach and back-up man stay near a side line fence. The fielder stands next to Ball 2. (Figure 91.)

When the coach yells "Go," the fielder runs to Ball 1, picks it up, and throws to the back-up man. He fields and throws each ball in turn, e.g., Ball 2, Ball 3, and so on. *Note:* Ball 5 should be a one-hop throw. Repeat several times.

(FIGURE 91)

Comment — Before starting play, demonstrate these skills for the player:
- Show a cross-seam grip. Point out how the ball leaves the hand with the same spin each time.
- Show how a strong wrist snap before releasing the ball adds power to the throw.
- Stress following through completely after releasing the ball.
- Emphasize making shoulder high throws to the glove side of the back-up man.

Time — 20 to 25 minutes.

156. Hit the Cut-Off Man

Objective — To give players practice throwing to the cut-off man.
Procedure — Place 4 balls 30 feet apart in a horizontal line. The fielder stands behind Balls 2 and 3. The coach stays near a side line fence. The back-up man, standing 30 feet ahead of the coach, acts as cut-off. (Figure 92.)

      When the coach yells "Go," the fielder runs to Ball 1, picks it up, and throws to the cut-off man. The coach lines up the cut-off man by shouting instructions, e.g., "Left, left" or "Right, right", and so on. The fielder picks up each ball in turn and makes his throw. Play continues with the coach hitting fungos back to the fielder. Repeat 2 or 3 times.

Comment — See Comments, Drill 154.
Time — 15 to 20 minutes.

157. Poor Throwing Catcher

Objective — To help a catcher make good throws to second base.
Procedure — A pitcher, catcher, and two infielders take their positions according to Figure 93. The coach stands near the catcher. Infielders take turns playing second base and backing-up throws. The catcher wears full protective gear.

      Action begins when the pitcher delivers a ball to the catcher. The catcher throws for a spot approximately 30 feet in front of second base. He attempts to

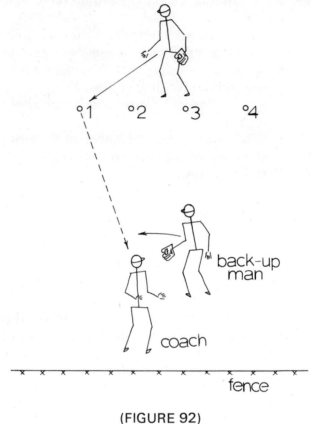

°1   °2   °3   °4

back-up
man

coach

fence

(FIGURE 92)

reach second base with a single bounce throw. The catcher adjusts his throw to reach the baseman about knee high. The catcher makes 10 to 15 throws to second base.

Comment — Show the catcher how to get rid of the ball quickly. A catcher with a weak arm can throw out runners if he concentrates on making accurate single bounce throws to second.

Time — 15 to 20 minutes.

Major Hitting Problems

Chapter 6 covered 9 hitting problems and ways to solve them. This section includes 8 additional problems that can lead to severe

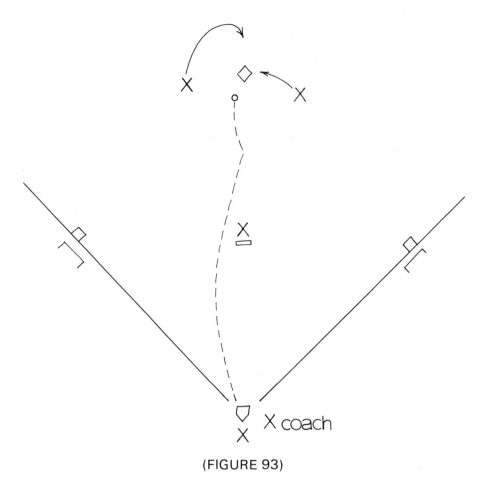

(FIGURE 93)

batting slumps. The coach is in a good position to help the hitter during batting practice.

158. Overstride

Objective — To keep the batter from overstriding.
Procedure — During batting practice, have the batter make these adjustments:
  • Spread feet farther apart and stand flat-footed.
  • Mark a restricting point with a bat, glove, etc., beyond which you don't want the batter to extend his lead foot.

- Place more weight on the back foot.
- Swing easy. Try to drive ball up the middle of the diamond.

Time — Varies with individual.

159. Lunging

Objective — To keep the batter from lunging toward the ball.
Procedure — During batting practice, have the batter make these adjustments:
- Take a wider stance at the plate.
- Keep weight back on rear foot.
- Wait a little longer before swinging the bat. Use quick wrists and hit everything to right field.
- Swing easy. Keep eyes fixed on the pitch.

Time — Varies with individual.

160. Jammed

Objective — To help a batter make solid contact with inside pitches.
Procedure — During batting practice, tell the hurler to keep his pitches on the inside corner. Have the batter make these adjustments:
- Open stance slightly. Move away from home plate.
- Use a choke grip on a lighter bat. Keep hands away from body. Bring hips around faster.
- Hit the ball out in front of home plate.

Time — Varies with individual.

161. Easily Fooled

Objective — To keep a batter from being easily fooled at the plate.
Procedure — During batting practice, tell the batter to make these adjustments:
- Step back a little from the plate. Get a better look at the ball.
- Choke up on the bat and swing easy. Try to hit the pitch up the middle of the diamond.
- Take a short stride, 5 to 6 inches. *Note:* Over-

striding causes body weight to shift to the front foot. This shifting causes the batter to lose power.

Time — Varies with individual.

162. Back Foot in Motion

Objective — To keep the batter from moving his back foot.
Procedure — During batting practice, have the batter make these adjustments:
- Place more weight on the rear foot.
- Choke up and swing easy.
- Wait a little longer and hit to the opposite field.

Time — Varies with individual.

163. Weak Curve Ball Hitter

Objective — To help the batter hit the curve ball.
Procedure — During batting practice, tell the hurler to throw curve balls. Have the batter make these adjustments:
- Straighten body and shorten stance.
- Keep front shoulder pointing at the ball.
- Follow ball all of the way into the catcher's mitt.
- Hit the ball to the opposite field.

Time — Varies with individual.

Most successful hitters have 4 things in common: (a) quick hands and wrists; (b) proper distribution of body weight; (c) knowledge of strike zone; (d) a swing that covers home plate. Developing quick hands and wrists require long hours of practice. Offer players the following suggestions:

- Swing 25 to 50 times at imaginary pitches with a heavy bat (40 ounces) or a leaded bat. Repeat several times daily.
- Roll a 5-pound weight up and down. Repeat 10 to 15 times daily.
- Do wrist curls with a 15-pound barbell. Start with 15 repetitions. Gradually add repetitions with each workout.
- Alternate squeezing a soft rubber ball or tennis ball with each hand. After 20 to 25 squeezes, change hands. Repeat 2 or 3 times daily. Gradually add repetitions with each workout.
- Alternate push-ups with pull-ups. Gradually add repetitions with each workout.

- Alternate squeezing hand grips with each hand. After 15 to 20 squeezes, change hands. Repeat 2 or 3 times daily. Gradually add repetitions with each workout. *Note:* Switch off between squeezing a ball and hand grips.

If a player fails to follow-through with a level swing, check his hands. He may be gripping the bat too tight, thus restricting free wrist movement. Give players these points:

- Lay bat handle near the base of the fingers. (Figure 94.) Wrap both hands around the bat. Line up the middle knuckles of each hand. (Figure 95.) *Note:* When a batter fails to line up the middle knuckles, he binds his wrists. (Figure 96.) A smart hurler will throw pitches on the inside corner. He knows the batter will have trouble making contact.
- A firm, but relaxed grip allows the hitter to bring the bat around easier. (Figures 97A, 97B, 97C.)

(FIGURE 94)

(FIGURE 95)

(FIGURE 96)

(FIGURE 97A)   (FIGURE 97B)

(FIGURE 97C)

11

Game-Winning Offensive and Defensive Drills

The only way to win baseball games is to score more runs than your opponent. A poor hitting team needs a strong defense with players who can bunt and steal bases. Conversely, a powerful hitting team usually does its damage with the "big rally."

The type of offensive strategy a team uses depends on several factors. These include:

- Player speed — Are they good base stealers? Do they hit into many double plays?
- Hitting ability of athletes — Do players make solid contact with the ball? Do they strike out often?
- Defensive strength — How many errors, physical and mental, does the team average per game?
- Pitching strength — Do pitchers allow many hits? Are they prone to wildness?

The activities in this unit give athletes experience in planning offensive and defensive strategy. Here are suggestions for keeping these drills running smoothly:

- Thoroughly explain each drill. Players should understand how these activities will be used during the season.
- Make plans ahead of time. Set up defensive and offensive

teams before practice. Try to keep players at their regular positions. Let athletes trade-off playing offense and defense.
- Have the infielders and pitchers work out prearranged signals for pick-off plays. Also runners and batters should have prearranged signals for bunt, hit-and-run, and steal situations.
- Keep extra players busy playing pepper, catching fly balls, or working on sliding, hitting, or bunting skills.
- Substitute at intervals. Keep drills moving at a fast pace.
- Make sure players wear protective equipment at all times.

164. From First To Third

Objective — To advance the runner from first to third.
Procedure — The defensive unit, infielders, takes position. The offensive group stays near home plate.

Action begins when the offensive team sends a runner to first base. A batter comes to home plate. On a prearranged signal, the runner steals second and the batter bunts the ball down the third base line.

Offensive Strategy

Give the runner these points:
- Take a good lead. Break for second when the pitcher motions home.
- Glance back at the batter. Be ready to return to first on a pop up. If the batter misses the ball, slide into second.
- Watch the third baseman. If any other player fields the ball, stay at second.

Defensive Strategy
- Tell the third baseman to look at the runner before making throw. A quick look may convince the runner to stay at second.
- Have the third baseman try a bluff throw to first. He may trap the runner between bases.
- If the third baseman fields the ball, have the catcher cover third base, shortstop cover second base, second baseman cover first, and the pitcher cover home plate.
- Tell the pitcher to throw a high strike on a bunt at-

tempt. After 10 minutes, switch sides and continue play.

Time — 20 to 25 minutes.

165. Safety Squeeze

Objective — To score the runner from third.

Procedure — The defensive unit, infielders, takes position. The offensive unit stays near home plate.

Action begins when the offensive group sends a runner to third base. A batter comes to home plate. On a prearranged signal, the runner breaks for home when the batter bunts a ball into fair territory.

Offensive Strategy

Give the runner these points:

- Take a safe lead. Don't stray off base too far. An alert catcher might fire the ball to third.
- Walk slowly toward home. Break for home plate the instant the batter bunts a ball into fair territory.

Defensive Strategy

- Have the pitcher make 2 or 3 tosses to third base. Two things may happen: (1) The runner will be more cautious; (2) The batter may signal his intention to bunt by dropping the end of the bat or turning his hips.
- Tell the pitcher to throw a high strike if he thinks the batter will bunt.
- Remind pitcher to watch the runner during the wind up.
- If the catcher has a strong, accurate arm, have him bluff a throw to the pitcher and fire the ball to third. The third baseman must stay alert. Caution the catcher not to waste a throw unless the runner is taking a big lead.

After 10 minutes, switch sides and continue play.

Note: The batter and runner must work closely together. The batter's job is to bunt the first good pitch down either base line. The runner must be ready to break for home immediately or return to third base.

Time — 20 to 25 minutes.

166. Suicide Squeeze

Objective — To score the runner from third.
Procedure — The defensive unit, infielders, takes position. The offensive unit stays near home plate.

Action begins when the offensive group sends a runner to third base. A batter comes to home plate. On a prearranged signal, the runner breaks for home when the pitcher releases the ball. The batter must bunt the pitch somewhere in the infield.

Offensive Strategy

Give the runner these points:
- Take a safe lead. Try not to tip off the pitcher.
- Break for home plate the moment the ball leaves the pitcher's fingers. Do not hesitate. Go full speed.

Defensive Strategy
- Have the pitcher work from the stretch and throw over to third base several times. If the batter starts to square around or drops the end of the bat, he tips off his intention to bunt. *Suggestion:* Tell the catcher to watch the batter closely.
- If a squeeze play is suspected, tell the pitcher to throw at the batter's chin (right-handed batter) or high and away (left-handed batter). The batter will find these pitches nearly impossible to bunt.

Comment — Combine Drills 165 and 166. Repeat often.
Time — 20 to 25 minutes.

167. Double Squeeze

Objective — To score runners from second and third.
Procedure — The defensive unit, infielders, takes position. The offensive unit stays near home plate.

Action begins when the offensive group sends a runner to second and a runner to third. A batter comes to home plate. On a prearranged signal, the batter bunts the ball down the third base line. Runners break when the pitcher releases the ball.

Offensive Strategy

Give the runner on second these points:
- Take off at full speed to third when the pitcher

motions home. Round third and go home when the fielder throws to first base.

- Be aware of a bluff throw by the fielder.
  Give the runner on third base these points:
- Take a safe lead. Try not to tip off the pitcher.
- Break for home when the pitcher releases the ball.

Defensive Strategy

- Remind the pitcher to check runners and keep them close to base.
- The third baseman will have his back to the runner from second. The pitcher should watch the runner and alert the third baseman if the runner breaks.

Time — 20 to 25 minutes.

168. Hit-and-Run

Objective — To advance the runner from first base.

Procedure — The defensive unit, infielders, takes position. The offensive unit stays near home plate.

Action begins when the offensive group sends a runner to first. A batter comes to home plate. On a prearranged signal, the runner breaks for second when the pitcher releases the ball. The batter attempts to hit the pitch in the area vacated by the fielder covering second base.

A good time to work the hit-and-run is when the count is two balls and no strikes, or three balls and one strike. The pitcher must deliver a strike.

Offensive Strategy

Give the runner these points:

- Bluff a steal. Find out which fielder plans to cover second base. The batter, watching the fielders, will know where to direct his hit.
- When the batter flashes the hit sign, take a good lead. Steal second when the pitcher motions home.
  Give the batter these points:
- Concentrate on making solid contact with the ball.
- Try to hit the pitch in the area vacated by the fielder covering second.

Defensive Strategy

A well timed hit-and-run play is very difficult to stop. If a pitcher suspects a hit-and-run, he should throw a pitch the height of the catcher's shoulders (provided he has less than three balls on the batter).

Comment — Reserve the hit-and-run play for consistent hitters and good base runners.

Time — 20 to 25 minutes.

169. Double Steal One

Objective — To score the runner from third.

Procedure — The defensive unit, infielders, takes position. The offensive unit stays near home plate.

Action begins when the offensive group sends a runner to first base and a runner to third base. A batter comes to home plate.

Offensive Strategy

When the pitcher motions home, the runner on first breaks for second. He stops before reaching second. The catcher throws to the fielder covering second. The fielder takes the throw and either tosses the ball home or traps the runner in a run-down. If a run-down occurs, the runner on third creeps slowly toward home. He breaks for the plate when the fielder holding the ball is in a poor throwing position.

Defensive Strategy

Let the second baseman take the throw in front of the base. He is in excellent position to watch the runner on third. If the runner breaks for home, the baseman throws to the catcher. If the player stays at third, the baseman traps the runner in a run-down. Have the shortstop cover second base and the pitcher back-up the first baseman.

Comment — The score, inning, number of outs, hitting ability of the batter, speed of the runners, and defensive strength are factors that determine when a team should attempt a double steal.

Many teams use the double steal late in the game when the winning or tying run is on third.

Caution the defensive team to be ready at all

times. The double steal can come with no outs, one out, or two outs (usually two outs). A runner may break on any pitch.

Have a set defense for the double steal. Too many defensive variations tend to confuse the athletes. *Suggestion:* Scout ahead. Find out the type of double steal a team likes to use.

When expecting a double steal, have the basemen hold the runners close to the bag.

Time — 15 to 20 minutes.

170. Double Steal Two

Objective — To score the runner from third.

Procedure — See Procedure, Drill 169: *Double Steal One.*

Offensive Strategy

As the pitcher goes into his stretch, the runner on first takes a big lead. The idea is to get the runner picked off and caught in a run-down. If a run-down occurs, the runner on third creeps slowly toward home. He breaks for the plate when the fielder holding the ball is in a poor throwing position.

Defensive Strategy

The pitcher can check a big lead by stepping back off the rubber. He may either throw to a baseman or charge the runner on first. The pitcher may also back off the rubber and make a quick throw to third. *Note:* This play requires much practice. An off-target throw could be disastrous.

Comment — The intentional pick-off works best against a poor throwing, left-handed first baseman. When a run-down occurs, the runner on third breaks for home when the first baseman's pivot foot is extended toward second base.

As the runner takes his lead from first, tell the offensive team to holler, "Get back. Get back." A nervous pitcher may balk or throw the ball away. If the pitcher doesn't throw to first, have the runner walk slowly toward second. Force the defensive team into a run-down situation.

During a run-down, have the shortstop cover

second base and the pitcher back-up first base.

Time — 15 to 20 minutes.

171. Double Steal Time Delay

Objective — To score the runner from third.
Procedure — See Procedure, Drill 169: *Double Steal One.*

Offensive Strategy

As the pitcher comes to a set position, both runners break at the same time. The runner on first stops before reaching second. The runner on third stops after taking 2 or 3 steps. He should be close enough to third to dive back safely. The runner on first tries to get caught in a run-down. Both runners breaking at the same time may surprise the pitcher and cause him to balk.

Defensive Strategy

Staying alert is the best defense for a delayed steal. The pitcher should back-off the rubber, and either throw to a baseman or charge the runner on first. During a run-down, have the shortstop cover second base and the pitcher back-up first base.

Time — 15 to 20 minutes.

172. Delayed Double Steal

Objective — To score the runner from third.
Procedure — See Procedure, Drill 169: *Double Steal One.*

Offensive Strategy

The runner on first breaks for second when the catcher is just about to throw the ball back to the pitcher. If the ball goes to second base, the runner on third comes home.

Defensive Strategy

A heady catcher may bluff a throw to second and fire to third. If a team uses the delayed double steal, have the shortstop break to a spot between second base and the mound to take the catcher's throw. He then cuts-off the throw and fires home. Tell the pitcher to move out of the way and give the shortstop a clear view of home plate.

Time — 15 to 20 minutes.

173. Fake Bunt and Hit

Objective — To advance the base runner.

Procedure — The defensive unit, infielders, takes position. The offensive unit stays near home plate.

Action begins when the offensive team sends a runner to second or runners to first and second. A batter comes to home plate. The batter fakes a bunt on the first pitch. A good fake will draw the infield in. The runner or runners steal on the second pitch. The batter squares around to bunt and hits the ball through the infield. An alert catcher can stop this play by calling for a pitchout. He then fires the ball to third base.

Comment — Try the fake bunt and hit with no outs or one out. Use a prearranged signal between the batter and runners.

Time — 15 to 20 minutes.

174. Delayed Steal From First

Objective — To advance the runner from first to second.

Procedure — The defensive unit, infielders, takes position. The offensive unit stays near home plate.

The offensive team sends a runner to first base. A batter comes to home plate. *Situation:* The second baseman and shortstop are playing deep. Neither player covers second after the pitch. *Note:* The short-stop should run behind the pitcher as the catcher returns the ball. This move is especially important if there is a runner on third. A high throw or wild throw could score a run or allow the runner on first to take second.

Action begins when the runner breaks just as

the catcher is about to throw the ball back to the pitcher. This quick move may draw a wild throw from the catcher.

Time — 15 to 20 minutes.

Pick-Off Plays

Successful pick-off plays take considerable practice. Worked at the right time, they take the steam out of a big rally. Many teams use the count system and daylight system employing the pitcher, shortstop, and second baseman. Here are 5 additional pick-off plays that we have found to be very successful.

175. Pick-Off Play One

Objective — To pick-off the runner on first.

Procedure — The defensive unit, infielders, takes position. Baserunners line up near first base. Send a runner to first and a runner to second.

Action begins when the runners lead off base. On a prearranged signal, the pitcher goes into his stretch. He spins around and throws to the shortstop or second baseman covering second. The pitcher repeats the procedure again. The third time he goes into his stretch, he whirls around and throws the ball to the first baseman. The baseman tags the runner.

Comment — Two quick throws to second usually assures the runner on first that he is not the primary target. He may take a bigger lead and get picked off. Change runners often. Tell them to take a normal lead even though they know the defensive strategy.

Time — 10 to 15 minutes.

176. Pick-Off Play Two

Objective — To pick-off the runner at second.

Procedure — See Procedure, Drill 175: *Pick-Off Play One*.

Situation: No outs or one out, suspected bunt.

Action begins when the pitcher, on a prear-

ranged signal, goes into his stretch. The third baseman runs at full speed toward home plate, and the
shortstop covers third. The pitcher whirls around and
throws to the second baseman. The baseman tags the
runner.

Comment — The runner on second sees the baseman break for
home. He is baited into thinking the baseman is charging a bunt. He takes a big lead enabling the second
baseman to trap him off the base.

Time — 10 to 15 minutes.

177. Pick-Off Play Three

Objective — To pick-off the runner at first.
Procedure — The defensive unit, infielders, takes position. Baserunners line up near first base. Send a runner to first
and a runner to third.

Action begins when the runners lead off base.
On a prearranged signal, the pitcher goes into his
stretch. He makes a fake throw to third, spins around,
and throws to first.

Comment — A good fake will draw the runner off of first base.
Note: A pitcher must have quick hands, a strong arm,
and the ability to make accurate throws. If he is lack-
ing in these skills, do not let him try this move.

Time — 10 to 15 minutes.

178. Pick-Off Play Four

Objective — To pick-off the runner at first.
Procedure — The defensive unit, infielders, takes position. Base-
runners line up near first base. Send a runner to first.
Situation: No outs or one out, suspected bunt.

Action begins when the pitcher, on a prearranged signal, goes into his stretch. The first and third
basemen run at full speed toward home plate. The
shortstop covers second and the second baseman
covers first. The pitcher whirls around and throws to
the baseman covering first. The baseman tags the
runner.

Comment — The runner is baited into thinking the fielders are expecting a bunt. He may take an extra big lead enabling the baseman to tag him out.

Time — 10 to 15 minutes.

179. Pick-Off Play Five

Objective — To pick-off the runner at third.

Procedure — The defensive unit, infielders, takes position. Baserunners line up near first base. Send a runner to second and a runner to third.

Action begins when the pitcher, on a prearranged signal, goes into his stretch. He spins around and throws to second. The second time he goes into his stretch, he whirls around, fakes a throw to second, and fires to third.

Comment — See Comment, Drill 177: *Pick-Off Play Three.* Remind outfielders to back-up all throws to the bases.

Time — 10 to 15 minutes.

180. Combination Pick-Off

Objective — To pick-off runners.

Procedure — The defensive unit, infielders, takes position. Combine Drills 175 through 179. Find out which pick-off moves work best. Repeat them often until the pitchers and infielders perfect their timing.

Time — 20 to 25 minutes.

12

Setting Up the Practice Session

The practice session, like an automobile engine, runs best when every part is working. Here is a list of seven major elements that a practice should have to be successful:

1. Organization
2. A time limit
3. Activities that hold the players' interest
4. Fast-moving activities
5. Activities that stress basic skills
6. Variety
7. A positive approach

Let's examine each of these elements and see how they fit into daily practice.

Organization

Plan ahead. Make allowances for poor weather. Post the practice schedule on the gymnasium bulletin board the day or morning before practice. A player should be able to walk into the gym, look at the bulletin board, and know exactly what he will be doing that day.

A Time Limit

Be consistent. Set a definite starting and stopping time. The best way to bog down players is to drag out practice sessions to the point of boredom. Try to hold practices to two hours. You can do many things in a well-planned, two hour practice.

Activities That Hold the Players' Interest

An activity should be brief, beneficial, fast-moving, and challenging to keep players interested. For example, Drills 26, 34, 51, and 55 are less than 30 minutes. Each keeps the athlete hustling and rewards the best performance.

Fast-Moving Activities

Drills that contain running, fielding, and throwing keep athletes on the go. For example, Drills 32, 33, 36, 39, and 40 require a player to make an all out effort. An active player doesn't have time to stand around.

Activities That Stress Basic Skills

A coach must decide which activities will benefit his players the most. If they need extra work on hitting, Chapters 6, 7, and 10 provide drills and games for self-improvement. Chapters 2, 3, 4, and 5 offer activities that stress fielding, throwing, and running.

Variety

Don't, please don't, do the same thing every day. Dull practices give baseball a bad reputation. Here are some "famous" barbs directed at baseball:

Baseball players suffer from insomnia. They get all the sleep they need during practice.

A baseball player learns to perfect one thing: To stand flat-footed with his hands on his knees while chanting repeatedly, "Hum-babe, hum-babe...batter, batter, swing."

A coach who includes a variety of activities in practice makes baseball a worthwhile event.

A Positive Approach

A good way to instill self confidence and build a winning attitude is to include games and drills that reward a successful effort. Activities 55, 58, 59, 87, and 128 are examples of competitive-point drills that recognize an athlete's outstanding performance. Posting the names of drill winners on the gym office wall convinces the athlete (and others) that he is doing something important.

Here are some suggestions that will help you organize practice:
1. Hold a brief pre-practice meeting. Go over the day's activities with the players.
2. Begin practice with calisthenics. Lead the players through each exercise. Watch them closely. Make sure they bend

and stretch those sets of muscles that are used in running, fielding, throwing, and hitting. Try Stretching Exercises 1 through 6, Chapter 1. Include *Knees Over, Knee Spread, Shift Back,* and *Reach,* Chapter 1. *Note:* These exercises are not reserved for pitchers only.

3. Athletes need to strengthen their legs. Let them run relay drills. (See Drills 26, 35, 36, 39, and 40.) This is a good way to end practice.

4. Set up a program that alternates jogging, wind sprints, and relay drills. Running or jogging uphill strengthens the legs. Keep running activities competitive. An athlete running against the clock or against another player works harder.

5. Have athletes spend sufficient time warming up their arms. Insist they make throws as they would in a game. *Suggestion:* Have them pair off, stand fairly close, and begin playing catch. Then tell them to gradually move apart and throw harder as their arms loosen up. Try Drills 27, 28, 29, and 30.

6. A strong, overhand throw is a must for the outfielder. Don't let an outfielder's arm grow stale. From time to time, set aside 20 to 30 minutes for throwing drills. Use Drills 78, 80, 81, 82, 86, and 88. If possible, have an assistant coach work with the outfielders during infield practice.

7. Athletes respond well to competitive team games. Look over the activities in Chapter 7. Each player practices hitting, bunting, base running, and fielding under game-like conditions. Fit a competitive game or two into your practice. If you find one that is particularly good, make it part of your repertoire.

8. Batting practice drags when players stand around waiting for the pitcher to throw strikes. Keep athletes busy. Study Drills 94 through 99. Notice that each drill gives every player an assignment. Find out which ones work best for your players and alternate them every other week.

9. Make bunting a popular part of practice. Let players try Drills 111 through 114. They earn points by bunting balls into fair territory.

10. Don't try too many activities at once. Go easy, plan practice time wisely, and keep things simple.

11. Plan workouts using both the offense and defense. Stress basic techniques at each position. Players must understand

that extra practice and concentration are necessary before they can improve.

12. Spend 20 to 25 minutes each day working on defensive and offensive strategy. Chapter 11 offers 17 drills that help players sharpen their offensive and defensive skills.

13

Games Your Players Will Enjoy

There are several reasons why a baseball player grows stale during the season. He may tire from competing in the same drills; he may become bored with long practices; he may see little value in doing something just for the sake of doing it.

How can a coach reduce fatigue and boredom in his players? Efficiency experts for large companies agree that short rest periods help overcome boredom. The same holds true for athletes. Players should be allowed to take periodic rest breaks. Rotating the practice schedule and alternating daily activities does much in reducing monotony.

The coach should set aside certain times for "fun activities." These are activities that stress relaxation. A good time to begin these is generally around mid-season or near season's end. Let's examine some of the games your players will enjoy.

181. Fungo Golf*

Objective — To offer players a change from regular practice.
Procedure — The procedure is as follows:

---

*Hoehn, Robert G., "Fungolf for Baseball Relaxation", *The Coaching Clinic,* Vol. 10, No. 2, February, 1972, pp. 2-4.

- Players pair off into twosomes. The coach or players pick partners. The twosomes should be distributed skill-wise as evenly as possible.
- Each player receives a bat and ball. Taped, broken bats make satisfactory "clubs." Old balls or all-weather, rubber baseballs suffice as "golf balls."
- The "holes" or targets are made from broken bats (Figure 98) and are pounded into the ground in different areas of the baseball field. (Figure 99.)

THE DOTTED LINES
INDICATE ABOUT WHERE
THE BAT SHOULD BE CUT.

THE BAT AFTER THE
HANDLE IS CUT AWAY.

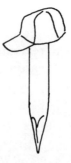

THIS SHOWS THE COMPLETE TARGET. A BASEBALL HAT
PLACED ON TOP OF THE BAT MAKES THE TARGET
EASIER TO SEE.

(FIGURE 98)

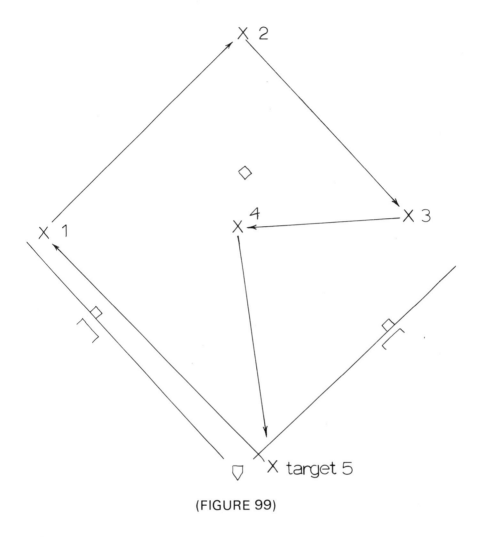

(FIGURE 99)

- Each player makes a score sheet from a 3x5 index
  card. He numbers the card 1 through 15.
- Players "tee off" at home plate. Each player takes
  turns fungoing the ball to the first target in left
  field. The ball is fungoed only once to each target
  (Exception: A player can "putt" or "chip" between
  the fourth and fifth target).
- A "putt" is hitting the baseball with the fat end of
  the bat. The player uses a golf swing in making
  contact with the ball. A "chip" is fungoing the base-

ball very easily. This is done by choking high on the bat. A "tee shot" is fungoing hard toward the target. The player picks up a ball, tosses it in the air, and hits it with the bat.

- After fungoing the ball, the player isn't allowed to touch it with his hand. However, if the ball gets stuck in a hazard, it can be removed and put in play. Penalty: two strokes.
- With the exception of fungoing the ball, the player must hit the ball with a regular golf stroke; i.e., swinging the bat vertically to the ground.
- Each player records his stroke total per hole (target) on his score card. All five targets are played per round before starting over. Each player completes three rounds or 15 targets.
- A player completes a hole when he hits the bat target with the ball. This can be from a putt, chip, or tee shot. After hitting the bat, the ball must remain within 1 foot of the target before the player fungos to the next hole.
- The starting twosome (pair number one) must reach the first target before the next pair begins play. This greatly reduces the chance of injury.
- All results are recorded on a Fungo Golf chart. This chart includes every player's name and his total score for three rounds of play. (Figure 100.) The player totalling the fewest strokes over three rounds of play becomes the champion for that day. A Fungo Golf champion is selected at the end of the season.

Here are the rules for Fungo Golf:
- If the ball rolls next to the boundary or outfield fence, the player can remove the ball from the hazard. The same rule applies for balls rolling into holes, etc. Penalty: two strokes.
- If a player swings and misses the ball, he is penalized one stroke.
- Any ball lost or hit over the fence can be replaced. Penalty: two strokes.
- A ball cannot be raised or placed on any artificial tee; i.e., dirt clumps, pieces of wood, etc.

FUNGO GOLF		
NAME	DATE	TOTAL HOLE SCORE
Alvarez	5/14	58
Lerner	5/14	64
Norton	5/14	66

(FIGURE 100)

- A player must hit the ball with the fat end of the bat only.
- Players tee off behind each target area. (Figure 101.) This is an imaginary area where players fungo the ball to the next hole.
- A player must complete each hole before moving to the next target.
- Players must not play out of turn. Each player keeps his turn, regardless of ball position from target.

Comment — Athletes quickly learn that success depends upon the degree of concentration. A player who keeps his eye on the ball will not be disappointed with his score.

Two problems arise. A baseball team may be too large to play Fungo Golf easily or there may be an equipment shortage. If two playing fields are available, these problems can be solved. A 24-man squad can be divided in half. One half plays Fungo Golf while the remaining players take hitting practice.

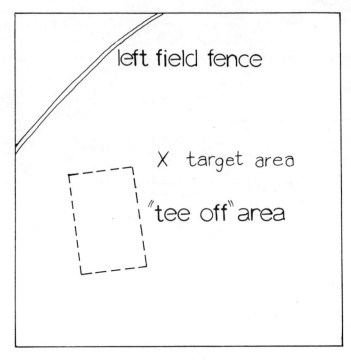

(FIGURE 101)

Twelve players can complete three rounds of Fungo
Golf in about one hour. After this time, the teams
switch and continue play.

Honesty builds the foundation of the drill. Since
there are no referees or official scorekeepers, players
control scoring accuracy.

Time — One hour or more.

182. Trip Around the Circuit

Objective — To offer players a change from regular practice.
Procedure — Divide athletes into 4 teams, 4 or 5 players (optional)
per team. Set up 4 stations around the baseball field.
(Figure 102.)

Action begins when each team goes to a different station and performs the scheduled activity. The
procedure for each station is as follows:

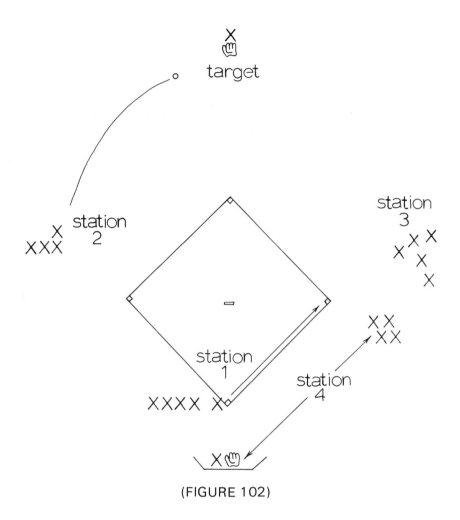

(FIGURE 102)

Station 1 (Location: Home plate)

Each player, in turn, brings a bat to home plate, and assumes his normal stance. Another athlete, holding a timer, yells "Go." The player swings the bat and runs to first. His time is recorded on a card. (Figure 103.) Repeat the procedure twice. Have players time one another from home plate to second base, and all the way around the bases. Tell them to average the 3 times and record on the scoring card.

Station 2 (Location: Left field)

Place a glove in deep center field. Have players

STATION 1					
PLAYER	HOME TO FIRST	HOME TO SECOND	CIRCLE BASES	AVERAGE TIME	POINTS

(FIGURE 103)

take turns fungoing a ball to the glove. Another athlete, standing by the glove, measures the distance between the ball and glove. The distance is recorded on a card. (Figure 104.) Athletes receive 2 fungos. Have them average the 2 measurements and record on the scoring card.

Station 3 (Location: Right field, near side line fence)

Athletes position themselves according to Figure 105. Use old towels or rags for base lines. Player 1, pitcher, throws one-half speed to Player 2, batter. The batter receives 3 chances to bunt the ball. Players 3, 4, or 5, fielders, measure the distance between the ball and base line target. Have them average the 2 measurements and record on the scoring card. (Figure 106.)

STATION 2				
PLAYER	FUNGO ONE	FUNGO TWO	AVERAGE DISTANCE	POINTS

(FIGURE 104)

(FIGURE 105)

STATION 3

PLAYER	BUNT ONE	BUNT TWO	BUNT THREE	AVERAGE DISTANCE	POINTS

(FIGURE 106)

Station 4 (Location: Between first base and the backstop)

Place a glove approximately 150 feet away from the group. A player stands near the glove. Another athlete, standing 150 feet away, makes an underhand toss toward the glove. The athlete continues to toss or roll the ball until it lands in the pocket of the glove. The number of rolls or tosses are recorded on a card. (Figure 107.) Athletes repeat the procedure two times. Have them average the number of tosses for both trials and record on the scoring card.

Give athletes these rules for each station:
Station 1
- If a player misses a base or fails to hustle (as judged by his teammates), he comes in last.
- Require athletes to take a full cut. Start timer when the bat hits the ground.

Station 2
- Allow each player one swing per fungo.

STATION 4				
PLAYER	TOSS ONE	TOSS TWO	AVERAGE NUMBER OF TOSSES	POINTS

(FIGURE 107)

- If a player misses or fouls the ball, he receives a score of 150 feet.

Station 3

- Count only balls bunted into fair territory.
- Do not penalize batter for pitches fouled or missed.

Station 4

- Athlete must release ball from a point between the shoulders and knees.
- A player can not pick up the ball until it stops rolling.

Comment — The coach keeps time. He gives each group 15 minutes to complete the activity. After that time, athletes move to the next station.

Players like to improve their scores. Sometimes this leads to confusion. Avoid problems by not letting athletes keep their own scores. Have them exchange cards and rely on each other's honesty.

Hold a preliminary meeting. Pass out 4 score cards per player (3x5 index cards) and pencils. *Note:* Save time. Make up cards ahead of time. Explain the rules and how to keep score. Have athletes award points in this manner: 10 points for first place; 7

points for second place; 5 points for third place; 3 points for fourth place; 1 point for fifth place.

Determine a champion. Post his name on the gymnasium wall.

Time — One hour or more.

183. Ballympics

Objective — To offer players a change from regular practice.
Procedure — Divide athletes into 3 teams, 6 or 7 players (optional) per team. Set up 3 stations around the baseball field. (Figure 108.)

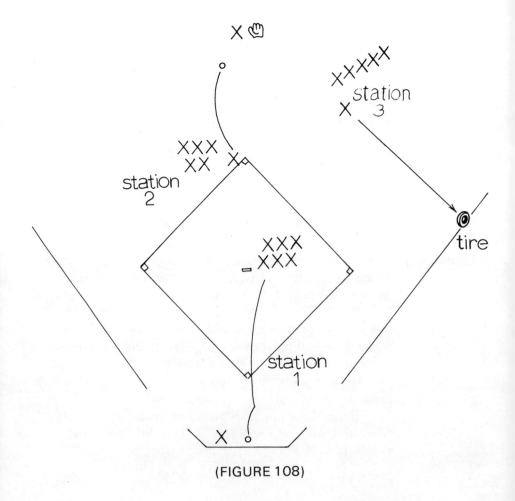

(FIGURE 108)

Action begins when each team goes to a different station and performs the scheduled activity. The procedure for each station is as follows:

Station 1 (Location: Pitcher's mound and backstop)

Athletes stand to the right of the mound and take turns fungoing balls into the backstop. A player stays near the backstop.

Each player receives 4 swings. He must hit 2 single bouncers into the backstop and 2 double bouncers into the backstop. Have players record and average the number of successful hits on a scoring card. (Figure 109.)

STATION 1				
PLAYER	SINGLE BOUNCER	DOUBLE BOUNCER	AVERAGE SUCCESSFUL HITS	POINTS

(FIGURE 109)

Station 2 (Location: Second base)

A player goes to deep center field and stands near a glove. The remaining players stay next to second base. An athlete, with one foot resting on second base, fungos a ball to the glove. He hits the ball twice. After he hits the ball a second time, the distance between the ball and glove is measured and recorded on a scoring card. (Figure 110.) When all players have hit, they repeat the same procedure, and

STATION 2				
PLAYER	DISTANCE TO GLOVE	DISTANCE TO BASE	AVERAGE DISTANCE	POINTS

(FIGURE 110)

fungo to the second base bag. Measurements are recorded on the card.

Station 3 (Location: Right field fence or
                        side line fence)
Stand a tire against the fence. Athletes remain approximately 90 feet away from the tire. A player stands near the tire. He acts as judge. Each athlete makes 5 throws at the tire. He earns 5 points for hitting the inside of the tire and 2 points for hitting the outside wall. Scores are recorded on a card. (Figure 111.)

Give athletes these rules for each station:

Station 1
• An athlete must hit from behind the pitcher's mound. Penalty: one point.

Station 2
• If a player misses or fouls the ball, he receives a score of 150 feet.
• If a player fails to step on second base, he comes in last.

Station 3
• Do not allow players to take practice throws. Give them time to warm up prior to the drill.

PLAYER	STATION 3						
	THROW 1	THROW 2	THROW 3	THROW 4	THROW 5	AVERAGE POINTS	POINTS

(FIGURE 111)

- A player can not take more than two steps forward. Penalty: one point.
- A player must use a three-quarters or overhand throw. Penalty: one point.
- If a player steps over the throwing line, his throw doesn't count.

Comment — See Comment, Drill 182.

Time — One hour.

184. Slo-Pitch Game

Objective — To offer players a change from regular practice.

Procedure — As the season draws to a close, challenge the faculty to a slo-pitch softball game. We've found that the student body and faculty show a greater interest in our baseball program because of this game.

We start things rolling by placing an announcement that reads something like this in the school bulletin:

The big moment will soon arrive. The mighty varsity baseball team will play the mild and meek faculty in a softball slo-pitch game to be played on Clancy Field, May 14, at 3 o'clock. The faculty needs all the support you can give them. Come out and watch the faculty cry and beg for mercy. Admission: No charge.

The physical education department can lend rubber bases, extra gloves, bats, and balls. Set up a diamond with bases 40 feet apart. Use the following rules for slo-pitch game:

- Varsity athletes are not allowed to play their regular positions.
- Varisty athletes bat according to their positions, e.g., pitcher first, catcher second, first baseman third, and so on.
- A team can have no more than 10 players on the field. The tenth man, rover, may play anywhere in the outfield.
- Teams must use softball equipment only.
- Players must wear shoes at all times.
- No leading off or stealing allowed.
- No intentional walks allowed.
- No bunting allowed.
- The pitcher must use an underhand delivery. The ball must travel through an arc of no more than 10 feet.
- A batter receives 3 strikes. If he fouls the third strike, he's out.
- Regular baseball rules apply.

Comment — Let extra players umpire until they enter the game. Make sure every athlete plays at least half of the game.

Time — One hour or more.

Index